The
Ultimate Adventure

Dana Grubbs

Written by Michael Wetzel

New Creation Press, Lansing Michigan

ISBN-13:978-1475247008

ISBN-10:1475247001

DEDICATION

This book is dedicated to all the hard working people who have been
downsized by corporate America, and have had to reinvent
themselves. My hope is this story will help encourage those people and
to keep them focused on their dream. Dreams do come true if you truly
believe in them.

-Dana-

CONTENTS

Dana Grubbs

I was at dinner in Conyers, Georgia a while back and a couple who were my customers came over to my table and thanked me for all I had done as well as how much they liked the store. I realized I had made a difference after all.

"What else is left?"

1 Do You Really Want It?

The dark water surrounds me as I watch the globules of air rushing upward into a tunnel of light. Suddenly, I feel a reassuring tug on my arm as Dana directs me to take off my dive mask. A simple procedure meant to test my open water skills; this is my last step in obtaining scuba certification. Dana Grubbs, my instructor, motions for me to remove my dive mask, replace it, and blow out the water. A relatively uncomplicated action fills me with trepidation. But if my mask were ever accidentally knocked off during a real dive, I need to know how to keep my composure. A flood of water blinds my vision for a moment, but within seconds of placing it calmly back over my face, and blowing the water with one breath through my nose, I can clearly see Dana giving me the okay sign. His calm confidence inspires me to enjoy the moment here in a Florida spring fed river.

Dana loves these excursions to Crystal River. Quietly, he prods each of his students to step from the safety of the pontoon boat into a new world of open waters. Calmly, he reassures each one that he will be right there next to them as they slowly descended into the depths. Up to this point, most students have only experienced the green clarity of a cement swimming pool. Each night we met for class, Dana patiently led us from buoyancy control, to proper buddy procedures. He took us from the security of an Emory University swimming pool, to the sunny Florida checkout dive. And on this day, the time has come to test the skills that our instructor has given over the past few weeks.

And here in Crystal River, Dana's dream is becoming a reality. Each time a student captures the skills of underwater compass navigation, buddy tows, or controlled breathing techniques, Dana knows he has gained a new world for himself. This is different from the old days at Eastern Airlines when he could only wish for something better.

Dana not only has the ability to dream a dream, but he has learned along the way some simple ideas for making it happen. He

3

has never forgotten those who still work at jobs, which frustrate them, making them wish they, too, could have something better in life. Dana knows that too many people sit listlessly watching others having great adventures. It was there in Crystal River that he not only lived his dream but showed others how to do it too.

This was Dana's aspiration; to get out of the nine-to-five rigorous routine and stand on the deck of a cruise boat at sunset with his own dive students; to sit around the cabana deck after a day of diving, playing his guitar, and listen to the excited rehashing of the days adventures by his newly certified students. For years he had only dreamed of starting his business, punching out the time clock,

and actually enjoying his work.

As a child he had watched Mike Nelson on Sea Hunt, a popular television series. Flipping backwards from boat to sea, Mike would unfold a new adventure each week, sometimes dangerous, sometimes dramatic, but always a magical time of underwater discoveries. He recalled that, "As long as I can remember I've wanted to scuba dive. I can recall watching Sea Hunt on television and thinking how great that must be. So, I guess during Sea Hunt the diving seed was planted."

Dana's dream of someday sharing the same adventures would come true when he became an open water diver and started his adventure. It was on a 1984 dive trip to the Cayman Islands with his family that he discovered he wanted more than an occasional recreational vacation. While diving with his only child, Angela, he realized how much he really wanted his own scuba business and decided to start moving forward.

But there were delays to his dream. There was a period when he wondered if he was just deluding himself, wondering if it would actually happen. Doubts began to set in as he entered the turbulent waters of personal crisis. It would be three more years before he actually took the first step to opening his own business. And it would be a total of ten years before he would actually open the doors. It was a long hard journey, but Dana never gave up. Where most of us would quit after six months of frustration, Dana found ways to satisfy his vision.

Sometimes we jump into the depths of the ocean before we are ready. We need time in the pool to get used to unfamiliar equipment. Basic skills like neutral buoyancy must be mastered before we can take on ocean currents. Breathing slowly and methodically through a regulator must become a natural process for us. Otherwise, when we take our first ocean dive and see that first Moray Eel our erratic and excited breathing may drown us. First things first. First we must pay our dues, put in our time and that is exactly what Dan Grubbs did.

We may think we are ready to dive into the big waters, when we actually need to start in a small swimming pool. This can be frustrating to us at first. Our desire is to head for the Florida Keys and do it now, but it takes time. How much time depends on many factors. For Dana, it took ten years of trusting and dreaming and struggling with life issues. Dana hopes the principles he has discovered will shorten your journey if you have been dreaming of starting your own adventure.

He tells the story of another man who had a dream and also followed a ten-year journey to find it. His name is Mel Fisher, a charismatic man who stood 6' 4" tall full of charm and wit. He loved to dance and play his clarinet and in his earlier days he was an avid scuba diver.

It was in those early years, while working the family's chicken farm in Gary, Indiana, that he began his own ten-year journey. His vision took his family to California where he opened his own dive shop. From there his vision led him to Florida to dive for sunken treasure.

Working with eight men called, "Real Eight" (a play on the term "pieces of eight") It was during the salvage of this 1715 fleet that Mel got wind of a shipwreck called the Atoche. Real Eight disbanded and the new company, "Treasure Salvage", began the search. Mel sent Gene Lyons (a member of his board of directors), to the archives in Seville, Spain. There, Gene discovered that the early scribes, who were paid by the line, intentionally embellished and elongated their work. This brought confusion to those seeking the whereabouts of the Atoche. Gene also discovered the difference in the way east and west was portrayed by the scribes. This information led them to the general area where the Atoche would eventually be discovered.

Diving off Key West near the Marquises, Mel Fisher and his partners discovered well over $300 million in priceless treasure. After ten years of searching, several bankruptcies, and the tragic death of his son and daughter-in-law in a boating accident, Mel's dream finally struck gold as buckets and buckets of gold coins began to rise to the surface. The salvage of the shipwreck Atoche continues despite Mel's death several years ago due to cancer. Ancient swords on the manifest haven't even been found yet. Mel Fisher went after his dream and paid a price, but in the end it was all worth it. Dana Grubbs also went after his dream, but it took some doing to finally jump in and go after it.

2 A Dream Growing Up

Many of us have a dream of doing something. Dana Grubbs did and so did Mel Fisher. In a made for television movie called, "In Search for Gold", Mel Fisher came before the high courts of the land defending his right to keep the Atoche treasure if he and his crew should find it.

He said something to the effect that a lot of people looked at them like a bunch of "raggedy dreamers". But he explained that he didn't care what they thought of him because when he grew up he believed it was all right to dream. Then he said something to the effect of, "That's what America is, a dream grown up." He felt that everyone should have that right, the right to believe in something and go for it.

Later on in the movie, after his son and daughter-in-law were trapped in a sinking ship and drowned, Mel was on the verge of giving up his dream. One of his friends approached him and told him it wasn't about treasure hunting anymore -- it was about the little guys who had a dream and felt like people thought they were crazy, but believed they could do it anyway. They looked at Mel Fisher, despite some public opinion that he was crazy, and saw him as a dreamer with the courage to continue the journey.

Like Mel Fisher, Dana had his own dream. And like Mel Fisher, Dana's dream spanned a decade of his life. For ten years Dana dreamed of owning his own business, being independent, while doing something he personally enjoyed. The obstacles have been great, losing a career with Eastern Airlines, losing his four homes, and a divorce. Starting a business with no prospects seemed overwhelming but Dana, a dreamer, but he found a way. Even though some looked upon His dream as irresponsible and impossible, he continued to believe and move ahead. He is a dreamer on his ultimate adventure. There were times when he wondered if he was crazy for not settling into the typical American societal lifestyle. The nine-to-five routine wasn't what Dana wanted. What he wanted was to join the ranks of those "raggedy dreamers".

3 Talking is Easier

For years he told friends, "I want to start a dive business". He even worked out some of the details of how he would begin. Even though he told all his friends about starting the business, he never actually did anything about it. In retrospect, he realized he only wanted to talk about starting a business. He didn't really want to take the steps. The dream seemed to be a mere delusion Dana held on to. Talking was easier. Dreaming didn't cost anything. Besides, he didn't know quite how to go about it. Cost of equipment, permits, facilities, and all the details of starting up felt overwhelming. So, for years he simply told people, "Someday, I want to start my own business."

It was easy for Dana to dream. It was easy to talk about his dream. It was like a mirage, an illusion that gave him something to hold on to during rough times. But when it came time to actually take steps, it was more difficult.

When we count the money in our pocket, begin to draw up the blueprints, and peek in the door, that's when most of us lay our dreams aside and choose an easier destination. Many of us capture an idea and think we can make it happen next week. After a period of frustrating roadblocks, we decide it's just too difficult, so we give up. Instead of taking it step by step, we want to leap off the boat into deep waters right now.

Dana remembered one of his first dives to Crystal River, Florida. "The day was beautiful with a slight breeze out of the West. The temperature was around eighty five degrees and for a September day you could not ask for more. We made our first dive about ten o'clock and I must say I was little nervous, but I tried not to show it. After putting on all of our equipment we were ready to go in. Now you must know that we had never tried to dive from a small flat bottom boat so you can imagine how everyone looked when we started hitting the water. My wife was in another boat and about fell into the water laughing at us as we were not too graceful."

Dana did overcome his nervousness and he and his team took the plunge. It was finally time to take that first plunge and stop

9

dreaming about it.   If we look out over a vast ocean, fear may overcome us. Looking at the big picture is important, yet we need not let it overpower our vision. Dana discovered, one plunge at a time, he could do more than just dream.

4 Keeping Your Head in the Storm

As kids we watched old pirate movies and saw, in the midst of horrendous storms, giant swirling of waters formed massive whirlpools that began sucking everything on their perimeter, including whole ships, into the depths of the seas angry darkness. Sometimes our own personal expectations can have the same effect in our lives. Swirling expectations can quickly overshadow our dreams.

One trip to Catalina Island illustrated this forever in Dana's mind. The boat with crew and team met with a storm on the way over.

"Some of the group was starting to get sea sick and have to make for the rail; luckily I was not one of them. I tried to close my eyes and take a short nap while the boat rocked and whined with the two inboard motors growling along in harmony. I am not sure if I fell asleep or what but for what reason, I was not sure, I realized the sound of the inboards had changed. I looked forward of the cabin when I saw a crew member from the wheelhouse go down stairs and open the hatch in the floor that led to the ships hole where the engines were.

The wind and rain were much heavier than before and the waves looked to be somewhere around ten feet. The boat would slam over and through each wave with an air of reluctance. You could hear the propellers coming out of the water as we negotiated each wave. At some points during the crossing the waves towered far over the top of the boat and believe me it was an eerie feeling looking out the window as we moved through the bottom of a swell and saw nothing but water.

As it turned out I was right. Something was wrong and one of the engines had quit. Most everyone on board was sick at that point, even some of the staff instructors were hanging over the side. But, for some reason I was okay.

It seemed like forever but finally we spotted the shore lights off the starboard side. Just then the captain came over the intercom and apologized for the trip and had us all sit down for docking. I had been on every kind of boat large and small but I don't ever remember when I was that worried about making it in one piece, but we did."

It took three years for Dana to finally sign up to become a dive instructor. He began his first lap with his trip to the Cayman Islands in 1984. Talking about it was so much easier, no responsibilities, no worries, and no investment. He had to come to a point where he felt he had to make a decision. Did he really want to follow his dream or just talk about it? Did he actually want to see it become reality? For years his thoughts about starting a business swirled in his mind as he weighed the costs ahead.

At some point he determined to face the raging waters trying to pull him down into the depths of funneling failure. Dana eventually began to sort out his priorities and focus on the dream in front of him. There was a whirlpool of obstacles between him and his dream but eventually his vision cleared and he could see the destination ahead.

Dana Grubbs

5 Fear of Failure

Dana could talk about dreams and expectations, day after day. He could let everyone know that someday he was going to open his own dive shop. He read the dive magazines, went on an occasional dive trip, and even dreamed of salvaging gold coins from famous shipwrecks. However, if he had not been willing to take the steps and pay the price, his dream would have never become reality.

He says he dreamed for years and years, but had to decide if it was what he really wanted to do. He had to decide if his dream was a mere delusion or if it was feasible. It could be that he just wanted people to think more highly of him. For instance, if we tell people we are working to become a movie star and have already had a role as an extra in two major motion pictures, they respond with "ooohs" and "aaahs". That pumps up our personal pride. Some of us become addicted to this sort of attention and never make a move into the next step. If all we ever do is talk about it, someday they will realize we are full of false hopes. Hopefully, we can recognize that before others do and save ourselves some embarrassment and energy.

These may be very noble goals. I have heard of people who developed pages of goals in high school and by the age of forty accomplished most of their list. But for many the fear of failure lurks in their minds. They have seen too many people try and fail and the "oohs and the aaahs" of recognition turned to taunts and ridicule. Many reached out for their dream and got bit by it and never tried again.

During Dana's PADI instructor course he was diving with a friend named Steve Shomer. On a compass run near Catalina Island, they were directed by their instructors to head out into a cove toward a sunken tugboat. Dana told me the story.

"We did fine going out but on the way in I noticed Steve dropped behind me several yards, settled to his knees, and looked at something in the sand. Suddenly he starts shaking his hand as if something is wrong. I looked and all I could see was a small hole in the sand. Steve starts doing his mouth like something bit his hand.

Since it was February it was cool and we had on full wet suits complete with gloves and hood, so I couldn't see his hand. When we got to the surface I asked him what was wrong and he said a lobster bit him -- clear lobster. At this point he pulled off his glove and it was full of blood with a hole through his thumbnail and out the other side. So I did a diver tow to the boat and got him to the doctor. The doctor told him a Mana Shrimp had bitten him. They live in holes in the bottom of the ocean and are real territorial. They have a tail with a barb. The barb had popped his thumb and the doctor told him he was lucky it didn't break his thumb since they had been known to crack the sides of glass aquariums."

Dana learned that if you don't know what it is, then don't touch it. However, that same kind of thinking held him back from his dream for a number of years. He had ideas to start projects like his own music store or make it big in real estate, but he keep wondering if he would get bit by some hidden issue he could not see or plan for.

6 Breathing Easy

One of the basic dive skills Dana taught me was to pay attention to my breathing. Always breathe. Do it slowly and methodically, no matter what. Once, while diving in Marston Springs, Dana saw a student forget this basic principle. He had just come back from California as a certified instructor and was working with another instructor.

"We were doing a basic mask clearing exercise. I was working with a female student I didn't know well, and was face to face with her. I motioned her to take off her mask, put it back on, and then clear the water. On her first attempt there was still water in her mask, so I signaled her to do it again. It didn't go so well and she panicked. Immediately she darted for the surface. There was a real danger of lung expansion injury, so I tried to grab her and slow her ascent. It happened so quickly that I only had time to wrap my hands around her feet and try to keep her from ascending too rapidly. At the surface, she was choking, crying, and cussing at me. I tried to fill her buoyancy control jacket and help her to float, but she was still too angry at me. I don't know if she was embarrassed or what, but she didn't talk to me the rest of the trip. Now, no one goes on a certification dive with me unless I'm sure they are ready."

The diver had totally forgotten one basic principle, to always breathe calmly and methodically. Her original problem was that she couldn't see without her mask. If she had continued to breathe through her regulator, there would have been no further problem. Instead, she was caught up in a swirl of confusion. Breathing underwater needs to become as natural as breathing on the surface. Otherwise, if we get into a precarious predicament, we may panic and lose perspective.

Dana learned the importance of slowing down, and learning to breathe when thoughts of failure and defeat swirled around him. He taught many students to remain calm and not fall into a panic when things begin to go bad. He learned this through his own experiences and has had to clear his own vision many times.

7 Clouded Dreams

My certification dive with Dana began in King Spring. It was only twenty feet deep, but the water was dark with a short visibility. For a newcomer, there were fears of what was lurking in the fringes beyond my visibility. Would some deep-sea denizen suddenly dart toward me with spiked teeth ready to snap off my arm or leg? I couldn't see far enough. My security was shaken. Descending to the depths below began a surge of distraction. I was more attentive to my fears than I was the experience in front of me. My mind began a slow swirling of confusion. However, I did breath – slowly – and once I made it through the dark water adventure and realized there was no danger, I moved on to the next level of my testing with Dana. Our dive the next day was in the crystal clear waters of Rainbow River. What a difference from the murky waters the day before. Below the surging surface waters a whole new world opened up. Green blades of grass flowed like a vast field of winter wheat on a warm summer day. I could see the breath of new adventure as schools of fish drifted by. Swimming was now effortless as we drifted with the currents enjoying unlimited visibility. Slow methodic breathing was easy here. The source of the river was crystalline water from a series of springs. What a difference from the day before. Now I could see clearly. My fear was gone. The clouded waters had been replaced with transparency. My thinking was not a swirling pool of confusion. Now I distinctly observed the beauty around me. I had no doubt as to my direction. I could see it up ahead. I simply relaxed and flowed with the current enjoying the journey. If I had assumed all diving was like the day before, I would have taken my mask, fins, and wet suit and thrown them into the ocean, giving up before I started. But, Dana assured me that there was something more up ahead. He gave me a vision of crystal clear waters and that's what kept me going. It was that vision that motivated me to finish the mundane tasks of my certification process.

Crystal Rivers are always flowing through our minds. There are whirlpools of darkened days, but we need to fight our way through those times. It is important to swim clear of all the bewildering expectations, lists, distractions, and look for those clear waters. It may be difficult at first, to tap into our true vision. It may take time. It may be a bit puzzling for us to discern our true desire in life. We must listen to our hearts for direction.

If we spend our time working in a cubicle office with no windows pushing paperwork for ten years, and find ourselves drifting off into a dream of starting our own lodge in the Rockies -- then maybe we should listen more closely. We may be wasting our energy trying to fulfill an obligatory journey when our heart is telling us to put on our hiking boots, flannel shirt, and jeans, and head west.

If we spend our days with dishwashers, washing machines, and lawnmowers, wishing we could start that home business, then maybe we just need to clear our vision and take that first plunge. Maybe we don't know how it will ever come about on our measly income, but we just can't get the idea out of our heads. Then maybe, just maybe, it's time to take that dream seriously and dive in. Granted, we do not need to leave our mundane job tomorrow ignoring credit card debts and car payments. There needs to be a plan.

Dana didn't suddenly come to the surface of his Cayman dive and decide to walk out of his career, but he did take steps. And he did listen to his dream and the voices of others who also had a dream. Even though there were plenty of obstacles he never drowned out the voices of vision he heard along the way.

One such voice was from a book called, "Chicken Soup for the Soul", written by Jack Canfield and Mark Victor Hansen. One of their stories related how Monty Roberts, as a senior in high school was asked to share his vision for his future, with the class.

"That night he wrote a seven-page paper describing his goal to someday own a horse ranch. He wrote about his dream in great detail and he even drew a diagram of a 200-acre ranch, showing the location of all the buildings, the stables and the track. Then he drew a detailed floor plan for a 4,000 square-foot house that would sit on the 200 acre dream ranch."

The story continued by telling how he presented the project to his teacher and received an F as a grade. When he questioned the teacher's response, she told him that his dream was unrealistic for such a young boy. That he had no resources, money, breeding stock, or any of the necessary needs for such a project. Monty was given the option of rewriting his paper and raising his grade.

After pondering his predicament for a week, Monty Roberts chose to keep his grade, and his dream. Years later he attained his dream complete with a 4,000-square-foot house in the middle of a 200-acre horse ranch. And then one summer, that same teacher came to visit Monty's ranch with thirty kids for a week.

Before she left she said, "Look, Monty, I can tell you this now. When I was your teacher, I was something of a dream stealer. During those years I stole a lot of kids' dreams. Fortunately you had enough gumption not to give up on yours." The crystal clear waters of the Caymans inspired Dana to one day have his own business. When his job with Eastern Airlines began to crumble he said his co-workers watched their careers crumble as the corporation swirled into closure. Everything told Dana to give up hope. His three rental houses were sold to pay bills, his financial future was lost, and his savings were all depleted. Dana remembered one of those times when he almost gave up on his dream. "Everyone was on the boat and ready to head back out for their second dive of the day. We arrived at the main spring and everyone started to suit up and I must say they got ready rather fast for new divers. I had told everyone that if they wanted to they could go into the sixty foot cavern one at a time with me or my assistant Lane. Lane and I had done this time and time before. We divided up the class and started the dive. After I had taken my group through and we had returned to the surface I saw Lane and one of the female students off to the side in the shallow water so I went over and that is when I heard the bad news. Lane had not checked her air and had let her run out while in the deep hole. They had to share Lane's air to the surface. This was totally uncalled for on Lane's part. I don't know who I was most upset with, him or myself. I was responsible for everyone not Lane so I assumed the blame."

On top of that Dana's girlfriend lost a $300 pair of glasses and Dana remembered that nothing really new happened on that trip worth talking about and said, "Someday I will laugh about that trip –

someday." However, he also remembered thinking, "I started wondering if maybe it was time to take a break for a while." Dana didn't take a break or quit and eventually he owned his own dive business and made a living teaching doing what he enjoyed.

It was his desire to share with those who have always had a dream that it can be harvested from the bottom of a crystal clear ocean like buckets full of gold. Whether they sit behind a desk all day, stand on an assembly line, or busy themselves with the needs of their families, there can be something more. Dana is one of those people who, starting from ground zero, methodically worked out his dream, one lap at a time. He has never borrowed any money, gone into debt, or risked financial failure. He simply ascended slowly from the depths of a swirling whirlpool, moved into clearer waters, and lap-by-lap he learned how to harvest what was there in front of him all the time. He knew it was there, somewhere beyond the confusion and dismal waters that tried to swallow up his hope. And despite inner voices that said you have no resources, money, etc., he discovered that his dream was not just another on a list of burdensome projects. It was not just a delusion that haunted his thinking. It was to become a reality. The dark waters of a swirling whirlpool didn't stop him from finding his Crystal River. He listened to his heart and made the decision to move ahead, whatever it would take. He would find the resources. He would overcome the obstacles. He would see it happen. Even if it took ten years to do it, Dana's dream would one day become that reality.

8 The First Lap is the Hardest

Dana knew he had a dream and that it was a good dream, but it wasn't until 1987 that he did more than just enjoy the view. Three years after a Cayman Island trip he started doing more than just talking about it, he signed up to become a dive instructor. This was a seemingly crazy thing for a man with responsibility. With three rental houses to take care of, a family to support, and a full-time job, Dana decided it was time to take the plunge.

Eastern Airlines had employed him for twenty-one years. To leave such a position and open a dive business was risky, especially since he lived in Atlanta, Georgia. The dive industry was flourishing in the coastal areas. But, Atlanta was landlocked, not a decent dive spot within hours. There were always the clouded waters of Lake Lanier, but budding divers want to see porpoise, and coral, and all that ocean stuff. So, the idea of beginning a dive business, recruiting students from the city, and surviving was a gamble. Dana was willing to give it a try. He was convinced that his dream was something he should pursue, the true desire of his heart.

Besides, Eastern Airlines seemed to be entering a corporate upheaval and Dana sensed that his long career could be coming to an abrupt halt. He wanted to be ready for it. In January, he cashed in his accumulated vacation time, all his holidays, and his savings. He enrolled in the only PADI (Professional Association of Dive Instructors), dive school in existence. PADI was recognized worldwide as a respectable producer of reliable instructors. Countries like Australia and South America, anywhere diving flourished, considered PADI a reputable organization. PADI is the largest of several diver certification programs and is responsible for certifying divers in close to 200 countries. So, Dana felt he had a reliable future with them.

In 1976 he had earned his certification as a scuba diver. The scuba certification process is required for divers to purchase compressed air and underwater breathing equipment. It requires academic sessions for diver safety and basic dive knowledge, pool sessions for practice using equipment, and open water dives to demonstrate proficiency with the dive instructor.

But, eventually he felt it was time to take the next step and train as a dive instructor. The timing seemed right. As an employee of Eastern he had the time and money to develop his plan.

Dana says, "I was making good money at Eastern, but all I did was clock in and clock out but -- it was boring." Since his trip to the Caymans Dana had achieved the advanced diver status and he had the required number of dives under his belt to meet PADI terms for instructor training. He was accepted into the program.

"I decided on PADI because it was the most recognized school back then. You could leave that class and could instruct anywhere in the world. Shops from Australia to Hawaii would call for instructors from PADI. You needed to be an advanced diver with a minimum of 30-40 dives, which I had."

He worked on a way to defer holidays to vacation time and headed for what was called the Gold Course in California. About 30-35 people started the class, but only 15 graduated due to the physically demanding course. Dana, who was 37 years old at the time, was the oldest student in the class. Still, he earned his instructor's status. He completed his first lap by educating himself as to the basic skills needed for his newfound profession.

One of Dana's watercolors

9 Building Confidence

Opening a dive shop incorporated more than just laying out big bucks and hanging out a sign. He discovered the importance of educating himself in his field. He had been a scuba diver for years, but in order to teach others he had to find a course which would give him the confidence and credentials to work as an approved instructor. He needed to move beyond the whirlpool of confused priorities into the clear waters of distinct focus.

Learning the basics created a new confidence in Dana. For years he stumbled around in bewilderment wondering why he couldn't get himself started on his dream. Dreaming was good, but when he finally decided to dive into the pool he discovered the tools he needed to master his trade. In the beginning he was a bit nervous as to what he would find ahead.

On an early dive trip with a friend to Crystal River, Florida Dana recounted his first experience with the Manatees he had only read about to that point.

"Our wakeup call came at five a.m., and we just had a few minutes to throw our gear together and make our way down to our flat bottom boat at the dock. The wind was blowing across the river and with the temperature around forty degrees you can imagine how we felt. At one point Marcus looked at me as though to say, 'What in the world are we doing this for?' To be honest I don't think either one of us had any idea what we were about to experience. As we approached the area I cut the engine because I was told that the noise would scare the Manatees off, if there were any there at all.

The sun was finally starting to come up over the trees in the East but the wind still had that sharp edge that cut right through you to the bone. We started putting on our wetsuits. Marcus had rented a full wet suit at the dive shop and I had my shorty wet suit which I soon realized was not adequate for this temperature. I thought I was going to freeze to death.

Up to this point I had been looking for something that would resemble a Manatee but there was nothing in sight. The girl back at the dive shop had told us to get into the water and be very still, so that is what we were doing – or trying to do. I could feel the cold water seeping into my wet suit from just behind my neck and then running down my back. Man! Was it cold and as far as staying still I was shaking like a vibrator.

We just laid there in the water, trying not to move. It seemed like forever, but then as I was straining my eyes to see, something was coming into view far across the springs. It was too far to make out but we knew what is was and I could feel my excitement building. Then all at once you could see the silhouettes of at least eight Manatees moving right towards us. Here is what we came three hundred miles to see.

It was an eerie feeling watching the Manatees move closer and closer. I looked over at Marcus and he looked at me as if to say, 'Wow, can you believe this?' After a few minutes all of the Manatees reached us and man were they great! All of them were in the eight hundred pound range and about six to eight feet long. One of the largest ones moved over close to me so I started moving toward it so I could touch it. Just when I ran my hand down his back it started to roll over so I could rub his stomach. He seemed to like this. Sadly, I could see propeller marks on their backs from fast moving boats. The Manatees move slowly and have to come up for air and that's when they get hit.

Well, I don't have to tell you we were having the time of our life swimming with these mythical mermaids. It was as if they had no fear of us. This went on for about forty minutes and during that time I forgot all about being cold. All of a sudden play period was over and it was as if the bell rang. The Manatees started moving away from us. As quickly as they came, they were now gone."

Dana had read about the Manatees and dreamed of seeing them like this first hand. His preparation paid off. Studying the process can be a first step in making a dream reality. It can mean the difference between constant frustration and calm confidence. Dana discovered that principle. For years he only talked of starting a dive business. One day he finally enrolled in an instructor certification course and it paid off. The certification course helped Dana build the confidence he needed.

One of Dana's watercolors

For years I dreamed of someday scuba diving. It was only a dream, until I signed up for Dana's certification course. It was surprisingly simple. Within a few weeks I began to gain the confidence and expertise needed to send me on my first dive trip to Crystal River. Classroom sessions instilled basic principles of using fins, buddy breathing, and the other essentials of a good diver. In the pool at Emory University I checked my pressure gages, strapped on my weight belt, donned my air tank, and stepped off the edge into the deep end. Sounds simple. But, it was during these sessions that I realized how ignorant and how insecure I was about diving. The fear of descending fifteen feet into a swimming pool sounds ridiculous for some. As I learned basic skills in the shallow end, I developed confidence to go into the deep end. There was a trust factor that needed to be developed. I was nervous about relying on all that heavy equipment. What if I ran out of air? Would I sink like a rock on the bottom sucking up lung full of chlorinated water until I passed out? All these questions swirled through my thoughts until I came to understand the concept of weightlessness underwater. As I developed my understanding of the basics, my confidence increased. Then there came a day when the pool wasn't enough, I wanted open waters and we headed for Florida.

Yet, even then there was some trepidation. Were there sharks? Alligators? Piranha? Would the water be clear or dark and foreboding? How deep would we actually be diving? Fifteen feet or two-hundred? All these questions were swirling in my mind as we prepared for our trip. Once Dana clearly explained our course, my fear subsided and my confidence swelled up in excitement. All it took was some basic education. Once I knew what to expect, how to react, and how to handle my equipment, I was on my way to the ultimate adventure.

However, once I completed Dana's class and finally followed him to Crystal River I shared in that same Manatee experience that began his ultimate adventure. I experienced the same rush of cold water in my dive suit, the same trepidation of waiting for the Manatees, and the same thrill of seeing these creatures first hand.

Some people forego the adventure. Their fear of the unknown overwhelms them. They count the cost of equipment or hear a few shark stories and quit the course. Some even get as far as their certification dive and let some unfounded fear cut their dream short. There are pitfalls of any dream. There are difficulties to overcome and there are serious issues to be addressed. But, if we learn the basics and master the skills, then our confidence carries us to new heights.

For many people these heights will never be attained. One reason is the lack of knowledge. They refuse to read, study, ask, or explore. Dana discovered the importance of shoring up his understanding and it moved him from simply being a diver, to being a dive instructor with a new confidence.

For eight weeks he rigorously studied, digested hours of class work, and fulfilled his dive requirements. Even though he was the oldest student in the class, Dana's vision pushed him to excel in his class.

One of his former instructors, Mike Kurchewski, told me about Dana. "Dana was one of those motivated people, always setting a good example. Starting a dive business today can be very competitive but Dana was highly motivated, had a great desire, and was a hard worker. I trained a couple of hundred students a year; I knew he would make it."

After completing his training, Dana was qualified as a Dive instructor and felt as if he was on his way to starting his own business. But, as he found out, there was more to learn on his journey than just a simple dive course. It would be years before his dive business would become a reality. Dana thought his business was ready to go. He assumed that his newly discovered information was enough to set up shop. It was only the first step. Signing up for a small engine repair course gives us direction, but there are still tools to buy, and the practical steps of testing out the principles. He thought it was time to open the doors and watch the customers swarm into his shop. That didn't happen. Like so many others, Dana discovered that normally it takes time. Talking about starting a dive business was easy, swimming the laps was harder. He was about to get caught up in his own whirlpool of distressing life changes which sapped all but a seed of his dream.

Hiking the Appalachian Trail

10 Finding a Way

Back home he hit a brick wall, life changing obstacles which would lead him to his dream, but in unexpected ways. Even though he had begun the process of education, there was still much to learn. He had jump-started his confidence by going after the training he needed.

He also decided to press ahead with life and find a way to get through those times when the direction was unclear. He suffered as all of his security was being stripped away. The way became so confusing that he began to lose sight of his vision. Then 1989, his wife Elaine, was in a car accident. Hospital bills were overwhelming. As a result of the accident, his wife's retina detached and she became partially blind. For months she was unable to go to work. Dana's free time was spent helping his wife.

"We spent a lot of time in and out of hospitals. I would come home for lunch and doctor her eye. She was out of work for seven to eight months. Finally, through an experimental procedure from Emory University, her retina was secured again. Eventually she recovered and returned to work. But the stress of the strike, financial failure, and long hours in low paying jobs took their toll. The marriage ended in divorce and Dana was left with nothing but his dream.

It was during that same year, that his father-in-law, who was a retired teamster truck driver, shot himself for no apparent reason. One month later his favorite uncle, Luther Grubbs, also died, followed by his father and then his mother some months later.

His personal life, finances, and his career all began slipping from his grasp. Since no one would hire him because he was on strike, he worked into the odd jobs which didn't leave much doubt that he wasn't happy with his life. His dream seemed to be slipping farther and farther away. It was at that time that his union, went on strike.

"No one would hire you because you were on strike. So, I took labor type jobs. First, one with a sheet metal company, then I moved over to a friend of mine who had a Fiberglass manufacturing plant. He needed a person to take care of inside sales. His business started to do poorly so I left there and went with a company called Tamrock, that was an inside sales job also. I handled transportation for all of their heavy equipment out of France, Finland, and South America. I learned a lot during that period, but I was working ten to twelve hours a day plus singing and playing the guitar in some local restaurants on the weekends."

The waters darkened as finances took a plunge. His three rental houses were eventually sold to pay off bills. He said, "I sold all my houses but one. I've always been a planner and didn't want to get caught short. So, I sold them one year before the strike ended to pay off my bills."

He had donated one of the houses to the union during the Eastern Airlines strike, for a place to rest, cook lunch and discuss actions during the strike. He made $400 a month on the picket line and his house payments were $325. The union was unable to pay him any rent but in the end they gave him a 1977 shuttle bus used for transport. It was well worn but Dana didn't really care about that. He was always trying to help his friends. It hurt him to see them losing hope and losing their dreams. Financially and emotionally devastated, they left the company and filtered into low paying jobs, losing homes and their hopes in darkening waters. In 1991 the strike finally ended and in February of 1991 Eastern Airlines closed its doors.

Even though he had attained instructor status, Dana says, "I still didn't really know how to start a business. So I stopped and went on with other things." All around him there were confusing signs. Eastern Airlines did indeed tumble into turmoil and for two-years Dana walked a picket line. Once per week on the weekends he walked with twenty-five people for eight hours a day. For a while the strike left Dana bitter with memories which clouded his vision.

Frank Borman (the former astronaut and president of the company), and Charlie Bryant, (the head of the union), had a dislike for each other. In an attempt to scare the union Frank Borman allowed Frank Lorenzo (a corporate raider), to come in and give the union the idea they were about to do business. Everyone knew that

Lorenzo had recently bought Continental Airlines, along with several others, dismantled them and put people out of work. Dana believes that Borman never intended to sell out to Lorenzo, but before anyone realized it Lorenzo had gained control of the airline. He began placing what were considered unreasonable demands on the workers in an attempt to force the union out on strike on March 3, 1989.

Many felt the brunt of this same action as the seniority rating was canceled. There were numerous injuries as older men tried to take on the physically demanding work of their younger days. Many were forced to retire. In fact, one of Dana's friends who were nearing retirement age, and who had a high seniority rating, was forced back into a job that he hadn't performed for years. Dana had helped him plan an early retirement. They spent time together discussing whether he should retire or stick it out with the company. Regretfully, about four months after they talked, Dana's friend got up one morning, took a shower, kissed his wife and went outside to the garage. There, he hung himself. Deeply affected, Dana decided he would someday find a way to help his friends recapture their dreams instead of helplessly watching them slip away into dark waters.

His friends have always been important to him in the process. On a dive to Key Largo, Florida he said, "My buddy and I hit the water using a giant stride entry and I'm here to tell you when the bubbles cleared away from my mask I could not believe my eyes. The water was as clear as it had been in Crystal River if not clearer. The colors were unbelievable and at one point in the dive I noticed that I had forgotten all about checking my air due to the fact that I was so busy looking around at everything. I was using up a lot of air, a lot more than my buddy so when I got down to 1,000 P.S.I. (pounds per inch), I was ready to start up to the surface like the dive master had instructed us to do, but my buddy wasn't ready. He had much more air than I did so then I was faced with a problem. I had been told to stay with my buddy and not leave him – so that is what I did.

Finally, we started back and he still did not surface on our way to the boat. I was just about out of air so I left him on the bottom and started back up to the boat. You can guess by that time I was quite frankly close to panic. I made it back on the boat and the dive master asked me why I came back without my buddy. I explained the situation to him, but one thing I learned from all that was you should always try to back up your buddy."

It wasn't until 1995 that he was finally able to open his own scuba business. From his long dark journey he carried the memories of friend's shattered dreams. Later on, Dana came up with the idea of seeing his story and discoveries in print. Something he could put into the hands of others like himself. Something that could give them some hope, some first steps toward finding their own dreams.

He knows the journey isn't easy. He said, "You need to be ready to pay the price. You need to do more than just want to talk about your dream. You need to be willing to walk through the fire and come out the other side." He knows from experience.

Despite the circumstances of his life Dana never lost hope. Most of the time it seemed an impossible task to take the first steps toward beginning his business. The distractions along the way never completely buried his hope. And one day he finally decided, this is it. Stepping forward, Dana began his journey, began his business, and saw his dream become a reality.

11 Inspired!

"Russell Burnett, city life guard, and Buck Carter, Grant Park restaurant employee, made history last month by being the first team to paddle down the Chattahoochee from Atlanta to the Gulf of Mexico. 'A lot of other explorers have tried it, and several have reached the Gulf,' said Russell. 'But river men down the line told us that all the other fellows had skipped some of the worst rapids by riding around them in trucks, or had given up before finishing the trip.'

The voyage began on September 9, 1921, soon after the city pools closed.

'Four of us started,' said Russell Burnett. 'The other two were Bill Califf, my partner as a life guard at Grant Park, and Luther Grubbs, a reserve life guard. We had two 16-foot bateaux which we had built ourselves out of yellow pine.'"

Luther Grubbs, Dana's uncle, and three of his companions braved the rapids of the Chattahoochee for a great adventure. The young men met with many challenges. Burnett foolishly tried to pin down a three-foot water moccasin, with a six inch piece of stick. It had slid out from under some shore line rocks. Bit on the thumb, Burnett was raced by his friends to nearby Franklin where they gained celebrity status. Folks in that area rarely saw a snake bit victim, but they were also enthralled by the boys spirit of adventure because they were getting ready to paddle through the Bush Head Shoals, considered the worst stretch of water on the entire river. After two hours, the young men set out again on their journey.

The journey was beset with moonshiners firing warning shots at them, low food supplies, and rough waters. At one point they were invited aboard the steamboat Barbara Hunt, by its captain. They enjoyed a sumptuous supper and later found out that there was an unwritten law of the river that travelers were welcome to eat on any boat.

Regretfully, one of their boats began leaking badly. Luther Grubbs and Bill Califf were forced to sell it for $2 when they reached River Junction. Then they returned home.

The adventure was only a part of Luther Grubb's lifestyle. He also owned his own motorcycle and was always on some sort of adventure. Dana feels that it was his uncle that lit the fire of adventure in him, to reach beyond the safety zones of life and follow his dreams. That spirit of inspiration has stayed with Dana throughout his own journey. Every time the going gets rough, Dana remembers the news picture of his uncle, sitting in a boat of his own design, looking like Huck Finn, on the Chattahoochee. It is this same adventurer spirit that led Dana to move ahead into his own uncharted waters. Fighting the turbulent waters of a new business endeavor can take its toll. Following any dream can stretch our personal limits.

Beginning a business is a tough endeavor. There are people who say it's impossible, it can't be done, and there are too many rapids to pass through. But Dana has learned that it can be done. His inspiration has kept him going through the rough times. When he felt like giving in, one more voice would prod him on.

One of those voices came through the 1996 DEMA (Diving Equipment and Marketing Association) show in New Orleans. Nationally renowned motivational speaker, Frank Maguire, gave the keynote address called, "Let Me Be Frank". Frank was one of the leading management communications consultants in the nation.

He told the story of his early years, and how he was struggling as a business consultant whose career had stalled out. A young 27-year-old Vietnam veteran came to him with an idea.

"I want to ship packages from across the nation into Memphis, Tennessee, and do it overnight," he told Frank. Frank laughed at the idea. Why would anyone want to ship packages into Memphis? Why such a limited focus. His friend said, "Look Frank, you're not going anywhere right now, why not join me and give it a try?"

With no money and only a dream they approached the Federal Reserve in Memphis and shared their idea. "If we can guarantee overnight delivery, will you use us?" they asked. The reserve responded wholeheartedly. Sure, if anyone could do what these two dreamers suggested, the Reserve would gladly give them a try. Then the duo asked if the reserve would write them a letter saying so. The

Federal Reserve gave Frank Maguire and his young friend a letter stating that they were on tentative contract.

Two men with a silly dream took the letter to Chicago and approached a group of venture investors. With nothing but a dream and a letter, these two men raised $55 million dollars and began a business called – FedEx.

From a simple dream, two men began a business that today holds 60% of the market and charges 40% more for their service. People have developed a trust in the FedEx guarantee and a simple dream has turned into a major corporation.

Frank Maguire, who was the Senior Vice President for Federal Express and Kentucky Fried Chicken, spoke to Dive business owners from across the world. He told them, "Guys, you don't know what hard times are. We ran out to those first planes to unload and only had sixteen packages." Yet those sixteen packages turned into a world-renowned business.

It is people like Frank Maguire and Luther Grubbs who have inspired Dana to follow his own dream. Inspiration is important. There are too many voices that say it can't be done, don't even try, or just stay where you are and never reach out.

The Appalachians

12 Equalizing the Pressure

There are times, however, when the voices are drowned out by the pressures around us. Frank Maguire said, "You feel like you think." Sometimes our inspiration fades and all we hear is the howling of the storms around us and we have to stop, breath, and listen for those far off voices once again. The voices of well-meaning friends advise us to give it up, get a real job, or settle down and settle in. Those advisors, along with financial difficulties, bureaucratic red tape, and a host of other pressures tend to impair us from hearing the inspiring voices which have so faithfully stirred our vision along the way.

Dana taught me a simple principle. On one of our dive trips I experienced first-hand what is called a "squeeze". As I slowly descended into new waters, there was an ecstatic anticipation of what I would see in this new world. At first, my excitement occupied my thinking. Gradually a subtle distraction set in. I could feel pressure building in my ears. The density of the water increased as I descended deeper. This pressure was pushing in on my ear drums. That was the squeeze that Dana told me about. Suddenly my attention was torn from my exploration. All I could think about was the uncomfortable pressure in my head. I was totally distracted from everything but that tension in my head.

The solution was simple. Dana had instructed me to stop for a moment, gently squeeze my nose, and carefully blow. If it didn't work I was instructed to ascend a few feet and try it again. It worked. Periodically I would stop, squeeze my nose, and gently blow again. This simple procedure allowed me to clear the pressure and continue my journey.

The same principle applies to our journey into new ventures. At first there is an intense excitement at the prospects of finally seeing our dream becoming reality. The voices of inspiration carry us on a current of flowing creativity and exploration. As we descend further into new waters there is also an increasing pressure. That is a basic principle. When we move into new waters, there will always be new pressures. We should expect it. Those well-meaning friends will encourage us to apply down at the local factory. Our distributors will pester us with late notices. Our checkbook will look like a dried up desert spring. All of these pressures will begin to dominate our thinking. Our head will pound with pressure. The voices of inspiration will give way to the voices of despair.

We can panic and swim back to the surface, or we can stop for a moment, release the pressure and breathe again. And if it doesn't work the first time, we need to ascend a few feet to a point where the pressure began to increase re-evaluating the problem.

For instance, if we are suddenly overwhelmed by frustration and feel like giving up we need to temporarily retreat and ask ourselves what's wrong. Maybe we purchased a truckload of computer equipment for new business and are now stuck with high debt. There is a possibility that we really didn't need a truckload. Maybe all we needed were a few basic pieces of used equipment, just enough to get us started. But the credit card was handy, offering a new higher limit of spending. We began to justify our expenditure by telling ourselves that once the business was booming we'd be able to afford the payments. A well-meaning friend even agreed with us. Everything seemed to flow positively toward our decision.

But suddenly as we continued our descent there was a pressure building that completely distracted us from any form of inspirational progress. The pressure continued to build as we mulled over the outrageous interest we were now obligated to pay next month. Something was wrong. What it was we could not define. All we knew was that we were now depressed. The pressure was too much.

That is the time to stop, and listen again for our inspiration and direction. We can always back track a bit and re-evaluate our predicament. Spend some time alone in quiet. Sit and think. Clarify the waters. Pick up your record of inspiration and let it saturate your soul. It works! Watch the pressure blow away. Don't allow the pressures to "squeeze" out your inspiration. Hang on to it. Relive it. Let it revive your mind, clear your head, and fill you with a renewed sense of direction. Then continue your journey into crystal clear waters.

13 Hang on to Your Inspiration

One night Dana was having dinner with one of his good friends, Loraine Gourd. Loraine had helped him in many ways. She had taught him how to barter for equipment through her organization called Tradebank International. But more than that, she was just a good listening ear. When the pressure began building, she could hear things Dana couldn't. That night at dinner Dana sat in despair.

"For some reason I was just about burned out trying to teach scuba classes. I cared less if I ever taught another one. I had let my dive instructor insurance run out and it had been about one year since my last class. Then one evening something strange happened. Loraine and I were having dinner at a local restaurant in Conyers, Georgia. The subject of diving came up and I started rambling on about some dive trip. After I talked for a while, Loraine said something that started me thinking about my life in general. She said, 'You know your whole face lights up when you talk about diving. You must really love the teaching as much as the diving.'

Shortly after that night I started working on the dive shop. I contacted PADI for a refresher course. Then I contacted my insurance company and was able to submit my $495.00 fee just in time to reinstate my policy. Then I began collecting as much dive gear as I could, but it wasn't quite enough. One day Loraine came around with about $2,000.00 worth of used gear she had collected on trade from some pawn shops. Things began picking up. I taught a few open water classes and ran a few trips to Crystal River, Florida."
At that point Dana began looking for suppliers. He attended his first DEMA (Diving Equipment and Marketing Association), show to check out the manufacturers, and worked on getting a location set up.

All this from a few words of inspiration. Dana listened to a friend who believed in his dream. Her words will never be forgotten. Dana remembers that night clearly. The pressure had begun to build. He stopped for a moment with a friend, grabbed hold of some inspiration, and let it blow the pressure away. It is Dana's record of inspiration that keeps his mind clear when the pressures mount. It is his record of inspiration that breathes new life into his soul as he continues his journey. Inspiration is of key importance to Dana especially when he began to swim those first laps.

14 Getting Started

Every journey begins with the first lap. Sometimes that first lap can turn the tide of the whole trip, ushering in disaster and despair. Dana's first ocean dive almost did just that.

"We went to the Florida Keys for my first ocean dive. I didn't really know anyone when I went out on the boat. They gave me a buddy I didn't know, a gentleman from Malaysia. He was very experienced, but I was a little nervous about the dive. After we descended and began our dive I started sucking up too much air. I was nervous. After a while I looked at my tank pressure gauge and realized my air was getting low. I had always been taught to head for the surface when it got to a certain point. I motioned my buddy that I needed to head for the surface but I guess he had other plans. He was there to enjoy his dive and didn't want to surface. He hadn't used as much air as me and wanted to stay down. On my way up I got tangled up in some fire coral which was stinging pretty good. When I hit the surface I saw the boat and started swimming toward it, but I wasn't getting any closer. I realized I was swimming into a current. Then, after swimming for a while, I realized I was swimming toward the wrong boat. Luckily, I was still able to signal my boat that I was in distress. I was so embarrassed that I almost gave up diving."

That was Dana's first step into the ocean. Excitedly he had prepared for his trip, checking his gear, clearing his schedule, and budgeting his money. He had dreamed of diving in the Keys and looked forward to his first ocean adventure. But the adventure almost turned into tragedy. For a period of time he almost gave up. That first step was almost more than he could handle. It wasn't long however, before the excitement returned, his fear subsided and he was back on the road continuing his journey.

He had talked about starting a business for years; he had even attended school for his instructor status. When it came to the actual process of opening the doors of a newfound business Dana still lacked the resources and direction he needed.

It took a while before he began mapping out his vision but eventually it dawned on him what steps to take. He remembered back in instructor school that, "One evening after a hard day I was laying on my bed just kind of letting my mind wonder while looking at a map I was assigned to make for class. All of a sudden I got up and put the map down on the table. I got out my drawing pencils and drew a whale just about a mile off one of the rock points there in La Gunia Beach. The whale was blowing water (spouting) up into the air, half in and half out of the water. Why I put the whale on the map is a mystery to me but I must say it gave the map a real nautical flavor. Later the guys saw what I had done and they started giving me a hard time because we had not seen any whales out there at all. However, on the very next trip to La Gunia Beach all of a sudden one of the guys started yelling, 'Look, it's a whale, and it's exactly where Grubbs drew it!'. Well I for one couldn't believe it but there it was spouting water into the air half in and half out of the water." As Dana's vision became clearer he would see the difficulties of swimming ahead into new waters but something just kept his idea alive. At times fear told him to give up; it was too hard, too dangerous, and just too exhausting, but his dream, his inspiration kept him going.

15 Deep Pockets Thinking

Dana said, "The real work began when I came back to Conyers and looked at all the cost and programs. I went into sticker-shock. I was overwhelmed. Just to open a bare bones dive shop I was looking at a minimum of $100,000. That's practically nothing, just necessities. I was really downhearted but my friends kept pushing and encouraging me to go on."

He finally realized that in order to start his business he would have to make some changes in his thinking. His first obstacle was to change what he calls, "deep pocket" thinking. This thinking had him adding up all the costs of equipment, a shop full of inventory, and everything needed for a full-fledged dive business.

"For the person with deep pockets, it was easy. All they had to do was call the manufacturer and tell them they wanted to open a facility. They would tell them, 'I have 3,000 square feet and the money to fund it.' It was easier for them. They'd go in with two-hundred to three-hundred thousand dollars and the reps would flock to their door. I still had to get the prices of inventory so I would know where to go. I also had to figure out overhead costs on basic things like electricity."

As soon as the manufactures representatives found out you had deep pockets there was no problem getting appointments. As long as you didn't have any competition close by they were more than willing to talk with you. They would even offer competition protection, offering their products to a select few in your area. But deep-pockets certainly influenced them and it frustrated Dana's efforts.

That was Dana's first brick wall. He was trying to do it like the big boys but without the cash to back it up. At that point he was lost and had to rethink his strategy. He began to understand the immensity of starting a business from scratch. One-hundred thousand dollars was a lot of money for a person who had nothing, no resources, no backers, and not a penny of savings. The dream almost died. But he continued on.

16 The Big Boys at DEMA

Early in 1994 he finally realized the only way he was going to get the information about how much equipment cost was to actually sit down with the manufacturers.

"At that point I decided I had to go to the DEMA (Diving Equipment and Marketing Association), show in New Orleans. The trick was getting in. I had contacted DEMA as an instructor and they wouldn't allow me to come as a buyer, only an instructor on a guest pass with no access to price lists. If he was affiliated with a store owner, as an instructor he could be allowed in as a buyer for that store. At that time Ocean Quest (the shop he had worked for as an instructor), had closed, and even if it had been open, I could only have gone as an instructor. I would only have had a guest pass. The manufacturers would not have spoken to me in regards to pricing and programs. If you had a buyers pass, they would. At that point I knew I needed to get in as a buyer."

Dana learned that there were at least five requirements to get in as a buyer. He had to be a dive shop owner, needed a store front, and had to present them with one utility bill to prove he was in business. He also had to present them with a sales tax number and fill out the form.

At first he tried to explain to them that he was preparing to open a dive shop and that he didn't know his location yet. That depended on how much inventory he would run.

Dana said, "The lady I talked to was sympathetic but said she couldn't do anything for me. Out of frustration I asked her which came first, the horse or the buggy. Then, I was back to square one. I didn't have a location and didn't know how to stock the store. I went back to the drawing board. The year before I had already opened up a sales tax number under the company name of 'Moon Shadow Enterprises'. I contacted the tax office and added my new name under that number. It was "Ultimate Adventure Dive Center."

Dana then called DEMA back and questioned them further about getting into the show. They informed if that if he could get "appointment letters" from at least two manufacturers to look over their line for purchase, supply a tax number, and produce a store front, then he could gain entrance to the show and acquire a buyers pass.

He began contacting as many manufacturers as he could. Out of twenty he was able to get two representatives to give him an appointment. Representatives from Caribbean Sports in Fort Lauderdale, Florida, and The Paul R. Sheahan Company in Charlotte, North Carolina set up meetings with him.

Next he needed an address. He was able to temporarily open his business out of a friend's office. Then he sent everything in to DEMA and was granted buyers status to the show.

At that point, all the doors began opening. Every vendor wanted to approach him as a potential buyer. He was able to talk with them realistically about equipment.

"Although I didn't know the right questions to ask, at least I had entrance to the show and access to every manufacturer. That meant I had access to every manufacturer's price list and catalogues. Over a week's period of time I collected every single catalogue offered, every price list, and every brochure from every travel agent. Now I had the tools to work with."

There were nearly six-hundred exhibitors at that show and by 1995 they had expanded to one-thousand. Dana had an arm-load of information. He attended seminars on such things as "A Buying Plan that Leads to Profits." Day after day he listened to speakers, talked to manufacturer's representatives, and scoured the product lines. He had gotten through the door and was beginning to take the steps needed.

"I went ahead and continually contacted manufacturer representatives I had met at the show. Since I was in the opening stages and had little cash flow, they wouldn't talk to me or sell to me. First they wanted to see my business licensee and a storefront. I had neither at that point. A lot of those guys even require that you send photos of your store and for good reason. There were a lot of guys that tried to start a business out of a garage, which undermines the big investors. I could understand that but it didn't help me out much. They would open up a garage and manage to find four or five sets of gear and end up selling them for practically nothing because they didn't have any overhead. Then the store down the street would dry up and blow away. Fortunately that isn't happening much anymore. Now that there are government regulations, and since diver manufacturers have clamped down, it has pretty much done away with those garage style businesses."

17 Use What You Have

Getting started was difficult. It wasn't a matter of diving in the pool and swimming one easy lap. Other swimmers made it look easy. But for a newcomer in the pool, it could be an eye-opener.

When Dana made his first ocean dive his dream overshadowed the practical realities. He couldn't just dive in, descend ninety-feet and swim like a seasoned professional. There were still necessary procedures that needed to be followed, like breathing slow and relaxing. But, at least he made the dive. At least he began searching out the steps needed to make his dream a reality. And in the process he began learning an important lesson, to take it one lap at a time. Since Dana didn't have deep pockets filled with all kinds of resources, he learned to use the seemingly small resources he had in his own pockets to get started on his journey.

A lot of us are like Dana. We get excited about our dream, even jump in the pool, but suddenly we see the immensity of the project, the high costs, and the time involved, the energy needed, and we think we don't have the ability to go on. The other night I had a dream after working on Dana's book. In the dream there were several of us sitting around talking about what we would like to do if we could start our own business. One of the guys in the group began telling us he would start a gourmet restaurant. In detail he described each food item, things I had never heard of, delicacies that made my mouth water. He became lost in his fantasy as he talked about services, decor, and delicate cuisine. But slowly I saw his continence change as he came back to the reality of knowing he had none of the resources needed to begin such a tremendously expensive project. Deep-pocket thinking set in.

Suddenly, in my dream, I sprung to my feet and shared a thought that had just come to me. I said, "Have you ever considered doing that for one or two couples?" My point was this. Set up a little beginner's gourmet meal from his own home. One evening a week he could invite one or two couples over to his own home, set a spare room with two or three tables, elegant decor, flowers, lace curtains, the works, and offer a specialty dining experience. From that small beginning he could eventually expand to a larger business.

It was only a dream and I had heard of this idea before so it certainly was not original. People have tried it and it works. The point is that he needed to begin where he was. Dana's ideas were beginning to sink in – even in my subconscious thoughts as I slept. Too many people count the cost of their dream and then run in fear. Like Dana's first ocean dive, they get nervous, suck up too much air, and rush back to the surface getting stung along the way, and are ready to quit. That's what Dana did back in the early nineties when he realized he needed a minimum of at least one-hundred thousand dollars just to open the doors of a decent dive shop. He assumed there had to be a full showing of manufactures supplies, stock diversity, a building in key location, and plenty of hot advertising. That's how the big boys did it. They went to the manufacturers, plopped down the cash, and opened up another "Dive City".

18 Resource Check

Every dive begins with one important step. You must check out your equipment; count the cost. The O-rings on your regulator need to be checked and replaced periodically. Checking the air pressure in your tanks is a must. And taking a complete inventory of your equipment is absolutely necessary. You may not have the fancy "grade-A" equipment of the guy on the bench next to you. But the procedure is still necessary. Everyone needs to take an inventory and make sure they know what they have for the dive. Whether we have top of the line or used equipment, we still need to be aware of everything we carry on board.

Few of us have deep pockets or the ability to buy into a major franchise, but most of us have some sort of dream. What is your dream? Have you always wanted to start a gourmet restaurant, a bed and breakfast, or publish a book? Maybe you would love to retire, buy a small yacht, and work on your water color painting. That was another of Dana's dreams but we will talk about that later. What is the desire in your heart? Is it to develop your own home business, get out of rush hour traffic, and set your own destiny? Could it be that you want to spend your days in some distant islands, diving on reefs, and showing others the joys of the new worlds?

Whatever your dream, you have to get started. Talking and dreaming about it are easy. Taking steps to educate yourself for the needed skills is necessary. But there comes a day when you need to jump in the pool. And you need to know, those first laps can be tiring. The journey is worth it. It will bring you satisfaction you have never known, if you are willing to use what you have and get started.

Dana asked me if I remembered the stone soup story. One stone thrown into a pot of boiling water stirred the interest of those passing by. One by one they threw in what they had, a carrot, an onion, whatever was in their pockets. The soup started out as stone water, but was transformed into a tantalizing meal.

Dana would ask, "What is in your pocket?" Maybe your answer would be a few hundred dollars from your last tax return. Maybe you have something you could sell? Americans are a cluttered lot. We have attics full of old fishing gear, furniture, t-pots, and a plethora of items relegated to the dust in the corner. Maybe you could sell the old bass boat? That's one of the things Dana did. He traded a bass boat for a van. He couldn't afford a van. He did have a boat that he was willing to trade for a dream.

What are your resources? Can you sell your car, save monthly payments, and buy a used vehicle. Could you possibly sell your house, or move to a lower rent apartment for a while? Dana lived in the back room of his storefront for an eight month period. Can you trade services with someone? Figure out their taxes in trade for their painting expertise. Bartering is big business and growing in the United States. It is a viable solution to cash shortage. Dana bartered, cut corners, sold possessions and came to the conclusion that deep inside his pockets there are a few pennies that can be multiplied over and over again.

Deep-pocket thinking almost deterred him from continuing his journey. It wasn't until he scrounged around in his own pockets and discovered creative ways to begin, that he moved ahead. Over time he has found ways to purchase used shelving from department stores, methods of free advertising, and a myriad other ways to start a business with little or no cash in his pockets. Dana knew it might have been easier for him if he had deep-pockets full of cash. He could have laid out his money, hired others to take care of red tape, and taken life a little easier. But swimming the laps strengthened his mind and creativity. It was tough getting started, but today his dream is a reality.

Ask yourself if you want to maintain the status quo all of your life and look longingly at your dream as it is carried farther and farther from you on the currents of regret. Ask yourself what you want to be doing in five years. Ask yourself - what do I have in my pockets right now. Dana asked himself that question. He took an inventory, turned the tide, and took the steps needed to get started.

19 Commitment

There may come a day when the storms feel overpowering. Dana Grubbs experienced many of those days. There were days when he felt like giving up and closing the doors, days when he felt he was struggling alone in the water just trying to stay afloat.

He told a story about diving with one of his dive buddies, a man in his early twenties. It was a night dive in Catalina and their instructor had warned them of a cave on the right side of the entry area and told them to avoid going in at all costs.

"We ended up at the mouth of the cave and I was situated a little above my buddy, instead of next to him. We both realized where we were when we reached the cave. Steve looks to the left and then to the right to find me. The water was murky. I was looking right at him and was about two-feet above him. About that time he shot towards the surface. When I got to him he was flailing around, had no air in his vest, was hyperventilating, and his regulator was out of his mouth. He was really out of control. I shot air into his vest. He looked at me with tremendous fear and all he could say was, 'I thought you had gone into the cave. I thought you had gone into the cave. I couldn't find you.'"

There are times when we descend into the murky night waters and suddenly see a black hole right in front of us. It is easy to panic, lose sight of those who encourage us, and shoot back to the safety of the surface. A more seasoned diver like Dana will usually stop and take a quick inventory at that point. A decision needs to be made, will we shoot for the surface, or will we continue on despite the feeling that we are alone. There are many days in the darkened waters when we feel like we are all alone. There is a sense in us that if we closed the doors, gave up our dream, that not one person would notice.

We feel like six months down the road a good friend could come up to us and say, "How's the business idea going?" They would be totally unaware that we were no longer in business. Regretfully things like this really do happen in real life. I've had friends come up to me and ask how the job is going. They don't realize that I left that job and moved into another field, five months ago. They look at me with surprise, and I feel the disappointments at their lack of interest in my affairs. There were days when even Dana's closest friends seemed to abandon him. Sitting alone in the dive shop he wondered if he should just close it down and give up.

We need to keep the accolades in perspective. We cannot build a foundation on the praise of people around us. We must be thoroughly convinced that we truly believe our dream. If it's not our dream then we need to let it go. If it is our dream, then we need to decide if we will continue on, even if it's on our own.

It would have been the easy thing to do; to just give up. Divorced, career lost, and with empty pockets, but he didn't. He chose to go on, one lap at a time. He started out with a handful of used equipment and built a thriving business for himself. Early on he simply talked about starting a dive business. His friends thought that was great and encouraged him. The attention was stimulating. But after a while he realized that all he was doing was dreaming. He said it was almost as if he was waiting for permission, or someone to take his hand.

The day finally came when he decided he would do more than dream. And with that, he began taking the steps necessary to see his dream become a reality. At times no one was there for him. No one said, "Atta boy Dana," or even gave him a pat on the back. But he forged ahead anyway.

Dana said, "There are times when your buddies are not there for you and you must make a decision to follow your heart." One such case was that trip back in Key Largo, Florida. Dana remembered again that time when he was teamed up with a diver from Malaysia who had been diving for many years. They hit the water with a giant stride and he said, "I tell you when the bubbles cleared away from my mask I could not believe my eyes. The water was as clear as Crystal River and the colors were unbelievable."

Dana became so wrapped up in enjoying sea life; Angle fish, Needle fish, Sea horses, and Barracudas, that he lost track of his air pressure. Since he was so excited he used up more air than his buddy who was more seasoned. Dana needed to resurface but his buddy had other plans. He swam part way with Dana but refused to resurface with him. Dana had to make a quick decision, would he stay with his dive buddy as he had always been instructed, or would he resurface. The decision was obvious. He left his partner and angrily re-boarded the boat having had to explain to the captain what had happened and why his buddy wasn't with him.

"I learned a lot from that dive," Dana said. "The most important thing is that you try to stay with your buddy. But, if you must break off, then go because you need to take care of number one first."

That experience left a bad taste in Dana's memory. But he learned an important lesson. You need the support of those around you, especially when entering new and uncharted waters. You never know what dangers lurk underneath the surface. Someone had even spotted a shark on that dive, but it left quickly. Supporting each other is a necessary part of our journey to the dream.

Dana emphasized that there are times when our buddies may not be there for us. They may have their own agenda, schedule, or desires. They may be insensitive towards our needs. And there are times when they will abandon us. It is at that moment that you have to make a decision. Will you continue diving? Or will you quit because of one bad experience? The decision is yours. It will be up to you to show the determination and stubbornness to go on. It's your choice; a difficult decision. But for men like Dana Grubbs, the determination paid off as he moved into new territory.

20 Destination Search

The determination to move on through the storms ahead was a decision Dana had to make. Once he knew what he was after he had to pull out his maps and plot his journey. This began an extensive search for the direction and his final destination.

Dana loved the inspiration of Mel Fisher and his determination to find the Atoche ship wreck. Dana put me in contact with one of the crew members, Marisha Wagner Moran. She told me her story and their long journey as they searched for the location of the Atoche, a sunken treasure ship, and its cache of gold.

"I was a long distance swimmer. I owned my own boat and knew the islands very well. I knew the whole area because I was on the water all of the time. There wasn't much to do on the Keys besides fishing, so treasure hunting was the natural thing to get into. Bob Moran, who I later married, was also added to the team. Bob is an excellent flyer and navigator so his skills were gratefully utilized in the search. One of his ideas was to take me up with a parasail behind my boat, a beautiful Thunderbird. We found the twin Atoche anchors under a mound of sand that looked like a sand dune. Earlier the team had found ballast from the Atoche. Later they found a bronze anchor from the Atoche. So, the ballast, my twin anchors, and the bronze cannon all formed a line which eventually led to the Atoche treasure.

When you swim a long distance you see a lot of the bottom and get used to seeing what is natural and what is unnatural. I had an educated eye as to what is natural underwater, because of my long distance swimming. I don't know of anyone who had that skill. When you are on top of the water you just don't see. You have to be under the water and you have to cover ground.

Say Field, who was an inventor and genius, had developed the underwater Magnetometer, a kind of giant metal detector which we pulled behind the boat. Once in a while the equipment would break down so we would resort to visuals again. I would snorkel and use a hydroplane board with two handles. The boat would pull me and I could dive twenty to thirty feet in my search.

We had searched for two years straight without one day off, so finally one day Bob and I decided to take a break and do some fishing. It was the first time we were alone together on Bob's boat, the Plus Ultra. One thing we always watched was where the fish were because fish congregate around structure.

We were on our way to anchor for the night when I saw all these fish and asked Bob to stop the boat. It was getting near dark, the wind was picking up, and the waves were churning. I shouldn't have even been in the water. Bob knew that and refused to stop the boat, but I just jumped in anyway.

I was looking for lobster but immediately found a small iron cannon in about 14 foot of water. I popped out of the water and started yelling for Bob and told him, 'It's a cannon!'

He yelled back, 'It's a pipe get into the boat.' He kept circling in the boat and telling me to get in. I refused and he finally decided to anchor, which was difficult because of the choppiness, and finally he jumped in with me to check it out. We both excitedly realized it was a cannon and settled there near that spot for the night. We searched until dark and found ballast, musket balls, and chunks of iron encrusted in choral. Eventually we found out it was a French or Dutch anchor from a ship that was probably looking for the Atoche. The next morning was dead calm, getting up to one-hundred degrees, a real scorcher. It was that morning that Bob and I found the anchor from the same ship.

We found the anchor and cannon somewhere between the discovery of the Atoche ballast and the twin anchors I found from the air. We figured this ship had been searching for the Atoche when it went down. So, all of this; the ballast, the anchors and cannons developed a line that led right to the location of the Atoche."

Today Marisha is now a semi-retired millionaire living in Tennessee. Her trained eye and past experience helped Mel Fisher discover the treasure of a lifetime. The crew couldn't just pick out any location. Time and money dictated that they move in as quickly as possible. The parasailing idea and their constant searching were successful. By raising their sights and getting a more broad perspective, the location came into focus. It was also important to have a trained eye, to know what to look for. Marisha didn't know how to find the location any more than Mel Fisher did. But they experimented, tried new things, and looked for possible signs. Dana Grubbs didn't know where his final destination was either, not at first. All he could do was look for the signs, explore the land, and expand his perspective.

21 Welcome Home

Dana told me that, "When I got back from the DEMA show my next step was to find a location for my business. Remember, I was working at the time; a full-time job. It wasn't that good. I was only making ten dollars per hour. So I was limited as to how much I could spend."

Dana said, "The term 'location' is important but not life threatening. For instance if you offer a quality product at a decent price, I believe people will seek you out. When I got ready to begin I took out a map of Georgia and one of Atlanta. I located every scuba shop and put a pin on the map. The demographics showed there were certain congested areas where shops were congregating. I picked a location and started my search. I finally found a place in Old Town Conyers which was a historical area. I was able to get the space for three hundred and seventy five dollars a month. That was for nine hundred square foot and was within my budget."

"I had looked for a lot of locations and couldn't afford anything on the four-lane interstate. It was too expensive. I could have swung the rent for a few outbuildings on the main drag, but they were less than perfect. I decided on Old Town Conyers. It had some recognition as the place to go. They hosted lots of festivals on weekends. I figured it would be a drawing card, 'Old Town Conyers,' verses, something like 2315 Harris Street five miles off highway 138. It had more recognition."

Ten dollars an hour wasn't much of a resource to begin a business. Dana would occasionally play his guitar and sing in some local clubs, but he still needed to find a way to open up his business. One option was to avoid the high cost of a new car payment. So, he drove an old van. Another high cost expense was house payments. That was no problem since he had been forced to sell all of his rental properties when Eastern Airlines folded. All of that profit was soon spent on paying off his bills. After his divorce he was resigned to apartment living.

When he finally found his location in Old Town Conyers, it seemed like a logical decision for him to move his living quarters into the back room of his new dive shop. Stuck back amongst dive tanks, regulators, fins, and weight belts, was a small cot for his bed. He had already brought his television in for classroom purposes. At night he would draw a curtain and keep lights low trying to hide the fact that he was actually living there. He wasn't quite sure how his landlord would react to that idea. But for a while it worked. The money he saved on home rent paid the rent on his new business.

22 Settling In

During the day he continued to work his ten dollar an hour job and at night he worked on renovating his brand new shop. He still hadn't opened it to the public because of the extensive repairs needed. He had found his location but he remembers the extensive renovations needed before he could open his doors.

"All I needed was a store front and a small area to work out of, and that's what I had. The store was a mess inside. It used to be a junk store. I continued to work my regular job during the day and cleaned my store during the evening hours.

That's where Bob Hatchet came in. Bob was another one of Dana's Eastern Airlines buddies and an accomplished carpenter. Bob would come over to Dana's new store front several evenings a week after working all day, and help him with the remodeling, even supplying Dana with some of the needed materials. Years back they had walked the picket line together for hours at a time. Now they were working to build Dana's dream. This volunteer not only helped build Dana's dream but gave him a gift he will never forget. Dana had little expertise in carpentry but he did have some experience in the rental business.

"The fact that I had a little background in the rental business gave me some good background on the renovations. I worked out several floor plans. I had owned five rental houses, so I knew what a landlord should supply when I looked for my location. He needs to cover all maintenance. By renting a storefront I didn't need to worry about the building as far as any major repairs. But this store was a mess. Because of that the landlord pretty much gave me a free hand in renovations. First I had to decide what department of business would bring in the most dollars and then I would decide how much attention and money to put into that area of the store. I needed a classroom (for dive classes), an area devoted to mask, fins, and snorkels, and areas devoted to other equipment. I had to decide where to put the counter and where to place displays so they would catch people's attention.

While I was at the DEMA show I looked over a few different floor plans. They know what is hot for the year. I even attended several seminars on store design. Some counters were placed near the front door, others were in the center. Some walls were designed in an octagon shape and psychologically moved the customers from right to left in a circular motion. That way you could control what they saw, at what point they saw it, and what would stand out the most. For instance, you would put your mask, fins, and snorkel (which are always the most popular) on the back left side. That way they had to cover three-quarters of the store before they got to them. My store wasn't that fancy. I had to modify, pick, and choose. I studied store layouts and marketing ideas in periodicals I received at DEMA."

During a seminar at DEMA, Dana heard the story of someone who invested five-hundred thousand dollars in their store. It was the Octagonal shaped structure. It had a pool in the center. Upstairs were several classrooms and offices. From the ceiling over the pool there hung a Manta Ray with lights shining down on the pool. Upstairs in one of the classrooms there was a glass ceiling designed to give the effect that you were underwater. A Dolphin tail and the head of another poked through the bottom side of the water; giving you the effect of being underwater and watching the dolphins jump in and out of the water.

He said, "I thought about doing that in my store. I would get an old rusted hull of a boat and secure it to the ceiling, making it look as though you were underwater looking up at it. There would be an anchor line running down to an anchor stuck in the floor. Then I would have mannequin legs with a wet suit on, hanging down."

It was a good idea, but Dana had only gotten as far as painting fish on his walls. He swore that one day he'd finish it. Still, he spent hours tearing down old panels, building new shelves, replacing carpeting, and trying to develop a presentable place of business. Again, he was on a limited budget, but found that he could do a little at a time and accomplish a lot more than he expected. He also came up with creative alternatives for setting up his business.

23 Piece by Piece

Dana couldn't swing $100,000 to open the doors, but he finally figured out a way to start – one piece at a time. He said, "When I finally decided to open the store (before the DEMA show), I had already started looking around for fixtures, furniture, slat walls, and display racks. I would hear of a department store closing its doors and end up buying a couple of racks or whatever they had. They would rather sell them than move them. So, I got some quality equipment for a good price. Several pieces were too big and a friend let me borrow his trailer. Whenever I could afford them, I would buy a few more racks and store them. All of my fixtures, my chairs, the slat walls, the racks, were purchased over a period of six to eight months. That way I didn't feel the outgo of money so much. So, when I got ready to lease the building, I already had ninety percent of my fixtures."

Dana told me, "One thing I hear people talk about is wanting to open up a restaurant in five or six years when they are more financially stable. The thought comes to my mind that now is the time to start buying stuff. Go to an auction, to a restaurant going out of business, and pick up a commercial blender, a slicer, or some other piece of equipment and store it somewhere. I don't care if they are an auto mechanic or a brain surgeon, if they buy a little at a time, when it comes time to actually begin their business they can have all or most of their equipment in place. I didn't even miss the money because I bought a little at a time, piece by piece."

"I learned to walk into a department store and ask the manager if he had any fixtures that he would like to move out. He would take me to the back of the store and sell me stuff he wanted to get out of the way. Some of them might be old chrome with some scratches. You won't get brand new quality, but if you are on a bare-bones budget at least it will get you started. I bought standard chrome racks and white slat walls and through some planning and searching they all match."

Furnishing his shop was not as difficult as Dana had imagined. At the onset he could have become caught up in the swirling confusion of deep pockets thinking. Imagining that he needed thousands and thousands of dollars for a site and equipment could have paralyzed his thinking.

There were various out of pocket expenses he couldn't avoid, like a three hundred dollar phone deposit. Yet, by paying his bills on time that was refunded to him after one year. He also had to buy a sliding credit card machine for two hundred and sixty-seven dollars. He accepted Visa, Master Card, and American Express in his store, but he didn't advertise American Express because it cost him too much. Every time a customer would charge on that account it cost him more than his profit could bear. He pestered American Express about that high rate of interest. He kept calling them. Finally they lowered his percentage a bit but not to his satisfaction. This was all part of the learning curve for a new businessman.

He also opened a personal corporate card through his business. Some inventory which customers purchased went on that card, plus some of his own personal charges. For every dollar charged on that card he received frequent flyer miles, which of course came in handy for his dive trips. He then opened a personal savings account for student travel fees. That way he could collect interest on the fees students paid him for trips until it came time to actually lock in the tickets. These details were all a part of setting up his dream. Once these and other details were taken care of he could open his doors.

24 High Ticket Location Savings

Like Dana, once you have determined what your dream is, and where you want it to go, you will need to decide on location. If you are beginning a home business the answer is simple. You simply need to determine the cost of any renovations, phone equipment, and office furniture. The obvious advantage of working out of your home is that public ascetics are not a priority. You can survive with rummage sale specials and meet clients at a restaurant or some other public meeting room.

Finding an outside location is different. Many of us decide to open our new business in the prime locations. Leasing fees are astronomical. For instance, Dana could have decided to open a store in the new mall going up down the road. A prime location indeed and there is something to be said for setting up in those locales. It can be an investment; a gamble. You might shell out hundreds or thousands of dollars in the hopes that you will draw in the clientele. You hope that your visibility will attract a large customer base.

That's a fine idea, if you have the money. Dana could have borrowed money, but chose another route. His decision was to go cash and carry. That meant looking for a location that wasn't as popular with the major leagues. Luckily he stumbled across that Old Town Conyers area. It was a lower rent district, yet it had a positive draw of customers to its old town atmosphere.

There are alternate options out there if you search for them. You may be able to buy a house with a large garage, or barn, or excessive space inside. You might be able to find living quarters that can serve the dual purpose. Some friends of mine were in the business of buying up abandoned warehouses and transforming them into living quarters. This might work for you in the beginning and is seriously worth considering. Sure we all want the full-fledged business we envision ten years from now. But, it might be worth avoiding the headaches of high debt and upkeep to begin small and swim slowly at first.

One Atlanta company set up a portable car wash and clean system using small trucks. They traveled to executive offices and washed while they worked. During the Olympics a major copying company revamped semi-truck trailers into a mobile copy center to work around the various Olympic venues. A mechanic that I knew purchased a station that looked like it should have been condemned. Yet, he had such a positive reputation as an honest mechanic that no one cared. His business flourished despite his location. Office space can come it at premium price. Yet there are alternatives. Some smaller companies have one or two empty offices used only for storage. They know the struggle of a beginning business person and are sometimes willing to rent out a space at bargain prices.

There are numerous options for the creative mind. Suppose you choose to open a small specialty muffin and coffee shop. Why not approach a local grocery store for a small space. Or gather other beginning business enthusiasts and lease a small warehouse or a vacant store front. Work together. If you choose to begin a car detailing business, why not approach a small car dealership for space on the lot. While you work on a customer car, they can browse the stock.

Dana was an innovator in this way. He had heard about a couple who lived in the back room of their bakery in order to save rent and get their business off the ground. This inspired him to do the same and to find the Old Town location to begin his adventure.

25 Bartering Organizations

Lorraine Goard, one of Dana's friends, had discovered Tradebank sometime before and introduced him to the concept. Loraine had worked in training and teaching upper management to focus, use their time wisely, reach goals, and goal planning. Her business was called Progressive Development. She would go into major companies and teach management how to make better use of their time, evaluate employees from interviews, and how to develop a management team. Eventually, the government began offering local colleges grants to do the same thing she was doing only for substantially less cost than she charged. That's when she began working with Tradebank International. Her goal setting and training skills became an asset in her new business. Being a close personal friend of Dana's, she began giving him valuable input on how to set his own goals and the intricacies of how to use trade dollars.

Loraine told me, "I worked with small businesses also. I helped them to set objectives and priorities and so I helped Dana ever since he began. You know, Dana is the kind of person who has all these long term goals, yet he has no time-table. He just does this little piece at a time."

That was one of Dana's secrets, to do one little piece at a time. His dream was long-term but there were pieces of the puzzle that had to be placed in just the right position to make it happen. One of those pieces was the financial needs of his business. That's where Loraine and Tradebank International came in.

As with most of us, cash was hard to come by. One thing that Dana desperately needed was a van. Transferring bulky scuba tanks and equipment back and forth to the pool for classes was an impossible task for a small car. He began brainstorming. What could he trade? At that time he owned a thirty foot travel trailer which had been his temporary home. Now that he was setting up his shop, he didn't need the trailer. He tried to sell it that summer but the market was dry. During deer hunting season he knew he would be able to get a good price, but he couldn't wait that long. He needed the van now.

A good friend, Bob Hatchet, owned a bass boat that he was thinking of selling. It was a nineteen foot Cimarron equipped with a Chrysler outboard motor. The outboard was not as popular, an inboard would have been more marketable, but the boat would sell. For years Dana and his friend had fished in the boat together but those days were past. When he asked his friend to trade the travel trailer for the boat, he accepted. His friend wanted a trailer for his lake front property and was ready to part with the boat. So the trade was made.

The next step was to find a way to turn the boat into a van. Periodically, Tradebank would hold a trade auction where items such as Dana's boat were auctioned off for trade dollars. Trade dollars could then be used to purchase other trade items. Loraine set Dana up at the auction. His boat sold for four thousand dollars. It just so happened that there was a van available on trade. Using his trade dollars, Dana purchased a 1977 Dodge conversion van for two thousand dollars and was able to put the other two thousand into more scuba equipment. The van wasn't a prize model, but it was what Dana needed. It had plenty of room for his scuba gear and ran great. On one of our dive trips to Florida the air conditioner would slowly ice up. It would develop a thick coating of white frost inside the elements and start spitting snow at us through the vents. It was necessary to shut it down until it defrosted, not a good thing for a six hour drive through the Florida heat. The thick shag carpeting covering the inside of the van was gaudy and worn. But none of that mattered. It served the purpose. He had his van. He could have purchased a brand new cargo van and painted "Ultimate Adventure Dive Tours" on the outside. He could have strapped himself down with outrageous monthly payments and captured an image for his business. Instead he decided to stay out of debt and stay with practicality. Rather than worrying about how he would make the next payment he was able to focus on the business end of his dream. He could have been caught up in a whirlpool of frustrating expenses. Instead he chose the clear waters of being debt free.

Dana says, "That is one reason I don't allow my vendors to put me on net 30 days. I don't even want to be in debt for thirty days. He wanted everything to be C.O.D., paid for when it came into the store. Eventually when the store was full of stock and it was moving well, then he thought, maybe he might go net thirty. That's only after he would have built up the clientele. He also got an extra 4% discount on everything he ordered because he paid on delivery. They give him the discount because they had the money in their hands and didn't have to wait thirty days to receive it."

That philosophy plus his trade options not only kept him out from under the debt that sinks most new businesses, but it gave him peace of mind. Tradebank was a way for him to extend the cash he conserved with his budget plan.

Through trade, Dana discovered a way to purchase the equipment he needed. Trade became one of Dana's key tools in developing his dream. With the help of Loraine and Tradebank Dana developed ways of finagling deals he normally couldn't afford.

For instance, he found that by advertising scuba certification classes on the Tradebank network he began to attract customers who normally would not consider the luxury of such a venture. A mechanic on trade would fix cars for other trade clients and accumulate trade dollars. When dollars multiplied, the mechanic, dentist, writer, or painter, would look for ways to spend. Seeing Dana's ad in the Tradebank newsletter, they decided to have a little fun with their money. They may never have considered scuba before, but now it seemed appealing. So, Dana began signing up students on trade. The two week class, including pool sessions, became an appealing draw in the trade community. Students signed up, took the class, and became certified scuba enthusiasts. Dana was then paid in trade dollars. Then he would turn around and use his trade dollars for the business.

Dana was able to use trade dollars for miscellaneous used equipment, store fixtures, and advertising. A local Penny Pincher newspaper allowed him to run ads in their listing. He printed up signs for the store, a sign for his van, and other forms of advertising. He was even able to take out an occasional client for a meal at a local restaurant on trade. Trade was a way to promote his business and still keep cash in his pocket. What we learned as children, the value of a good trade, became an asset to building Dana's dream.

26 Trading For Pool Privileges

There were other trade deals. Dana now had his shop but he needed a swimming pool for lessons. He said, "I also bartered to use people's homes and pools for trade. The person taking the class owned the home and pool and traded scuba classes for their use."

This worked when the pool owner wanted to get certified. But when they completed the class, the pool was unavailable. He needed something more permanent. Ideally, an inside pool for year round sessions would be great. Dana knew that most scuba shops don't have a pool, but if you want to be a driving force, you had to have one. For instance, if you aren't teaching someone scuba, you can offer swimming lessons year round in the pool to help offset the costs of owning one. Dana began his search.

"After I secured my store lease I actively looked for a pool to use in my dive business. I approached Oxford of Emory, a branch of Emory University located in Oxford, Georgia, thirty-five miles from Atlanta. I met with Seth Bussey, head of the intramural sports department. He proceeded to tell me his boss had just instructed him to find a scuba instructor, two days before I had walked in the door.

I then met with the dean of Emory and the head of the Physical Education department. We worked out the details of using the pool for class instruction and for my personal dive business. We came up with a comfortable fee for each student. That way they didn't have to transfer students to the main campus anymore for the dive classes. That gave them more control over the course.

My schedule was one night per week for a semester, from six-thirty to nine-thirty for one night of classroom instruction and a pool session the next class time. I began with eighteen students. Unfortunately I only had nine sets of gear. So, I cut the class and pool time in half with a time of one and one-half hours each session.

Oxford decided that each student should pay me $125, plus buy a thirty-one dollar textbook. I was doing real well at that point. But, when the first class rolled around I didn't have enough gear to do the class. So, I collected the class fees from my students, immediately got on the phone to my manufacturers and ordered new gear. I had a gear supplier that would sell me gear without a minimum order. The student fees supplied my cash. By the time the first class started, I was all set up. I continued this cycle and built up my gear supply fast. I was able to sell off some of my old used equipment, stuff I couldn't get parts for as easily."

Trade worked again. By trading his instruction to the college they allowed him to use the pool for college classes and his store groups. He not only obtained more students but also was able to snag an Olympic size, indoor heated, pool for the business. Once again, the bartering system preserved his in pocket cash and took him another step further in attaining his dream.

27 What Do You Have to Trade?

When I first came in contact with Dana it was through a trade deal. Dana decided to publish his dream. He had always wanted to do something for his friends who were forcibly retired from the airline industry and others like him. He knew there were many like them who had a secret dream but were not sure how to go about attaining it. One solution was to tell his story.

One afternoon he called me up and offered me a trade. I would write the book for him. He would pay me in trade dollars (from his scuba classes), get me certified as a diver, and provide equipment for my own adventures. Since I was a fellow Sea Hunt enthusiast I jumped on the idea. One year earlier I had moved down to Atlanta from Michigan. In my early days I had snorkeled in the inland lakes of my home county. When we moved to Atlanta I told my wife that I should take up snorkeling again. Regretfully, time and money hampered my dream. Then Dana called. Since I was a writer, and dreamed of underwater adventures, the idea was a winner for both of us.

I found other options for my childhood bartering fever. Dana was willing to pay me a finder fee on trade for any new student I found for him. I had also joined trade bank with my writing, a little company I called, "The Right Approach", and was able to get other trade deals like writing a news release for an advertising firm. I was even able to trade a deal for a trip to New Orleans.

Trading is a plausible way to keep cash in your pocket. Everyone has something to trade; baby-sitting, writing, painting, lawn care, legal services, dog sitting, and thousands of other ideas. Tradebank International and other groups like them are quickly expanding in our country. The bartering system is flourishing. Cutting out the middle-man, making a good deal, keeping cash at home, are just a few of the reasons people are flocking to this system.

Your personal dream may feel out of reach, especially if you are caught up in "deep pockets thinking". But, you need to look at your own resources and determine what you can trade. Once you begin thinking in that direction you will be surprised at how many options are available.

For instance, I know some hot fishing spots in Michigan's Upper Peninsula; I lived there for ten years. There was a lake near my home where I could walk the banks, hear the loons, watch an eagle, a deer, or a bear, and fish in seclusion for hours. It wasn't unusual to catch up to twenty mature Pike in five or six hours. I know the spot; very well. And many others like it. I have several friends that love fishing. What can I trade? These friends are willing to use trade dollars, dental services, etc., for a guided trip to my old fishing grounds. They get some good fishing and I get a good deal.

You, like Dana, may need store furnishings like shelving, racks, and display cabinets. Or you may even need a stock of inventory. Suppose you planned to open a restaurant. Dana's suggestion is to look early. Shop for good deals even years before you need them. For instance, a restaurant may be closing its doors. You discover a grill which would perfectly suite your needs. All kinds of trades could be offered from helping them to clean out the store, move stock, etc. Don't limit your thinking. Suppose they need a lawyer for some legal paperwork. You're not a lawyer, but you know a lawyer who would be willing to trade his services for your dental services, or writing expertise. There is always a way to make a deal. It is a networking process and may take some thought. But if you are short of cash and want to keep the money in your pockets, this brainwork may pay off in a valuable trade.

28 Salvaging a Sinking Neighborhood

Wheeling and dealing can pay off in the long run. You just need to unleash your creativity. An old friend of mine, Tony McCray, made his living as a Christian singer traveling extensively on weekends. During the week he developed a t-shirt business. He began out of the back of a garage but several years ago decided to expand. For around fifteen-thousand dollars he purchased a dilapidated house. His goal was to fix it up for his business. Rather than spend thousands of dollars on construction materials, Tony, a scavenger at heart, found a place where he could get free materials.

The local airport had condemned a whole neighborhood for future expansion. The homes where sitting empty. Tony obtained permission from a wrecking crew to go in and salvage all he wanted. He collected circuit breaker boxes, ceiling fans, molding, two-by-fours, paneling, bricks, and windows. Almost everything he needed to fix up his shop came from salvage, even counter topping for his kitchen. Using his creative mind, Tony was able to turn his fixer-upper into a beautiful business.

Creativity is the key to salvaging some top notch deals. It not only keeps cash in your pocket but there is something exciting about making a good deal. In our advanced society where we pay dollars for a handful of screws, good deals seem rare. But they are there if we look for them.

Dana has found some of those good deals. Good trades. Trades that saved him thousands of dollars and allowed him to begin a business that was once only a dream. Cash is not the only way to build a dream. Sometimes we need to break out of our years of focused thinking and return to the thinking of our childhood days. Thinking creatively, looking for the deals, working on alternative ways of financing our dreams can all pay off. Dana discovered how to furnish his store, stock up on scuba gear, and begin a business, by trading goods and services, searching for good deals and ultimately keeping the cash in his own pocket

29 Putting Profits Back In

Early on Dana made the decision to sacrifice. He chose to drive a used van paid for with cash instead of tying up hundreds of dollars in car payments over several years. He chose, for a period, to live in the back room of his shop instead of tying up hundreds of dollars in house payments and upkeep. He chose to do some of his clothes shopping at second hand stores instead of tying up cash in new clothes. Blair Smith, a dive instructor and travel agent who worked with Dana said, "Dana doubles, quadruples, checks every penny he spends. He is conservative in running his business and always careful to take care of his customers. One time Dana goofed up on not ordering a regulator piece for a customer. He just forgot. But Dana wrote a letter of apology because he felt so bad about it."

It's this kind of consideration towards those he serves and his careful conserving of cash that has given Dana the edge needed to start his business with nothing and watch it grow into a thriving endeavor. For many high-rolling businessmen with deep-pockets these sacrifices may seem insignificant. But for those who have a dream and a lack of resources, each of these and other ideas make it possible to move ahead.

When he secured permission with Emory University to use their pool and teach dive classes, Dana's first act was to take the student fees paid to him and purchase more dive equipment. His early profits were invested right back into his business. He has continued this process as his dream has grown. Larger profits from store sales have been used to purchase more equipment. Dana did not deny himself the pleasures of modern living. He had comfortable living quarters, reliable transportation, and was able to eat out and take dive trips thanks to his bargaining ability. Yet, these things were secondary. The first priority was to take a few pennies and build them into dollars.

30 Treading Gratification

Many people get a tax refund and choose to party down or purchase new toys rather than thinking ahead towards our dream becoming a reality. Dana, on the other hand, chose a different route. He chose the path of sacrifice. He was just foolish enough to believe that if he made sacrifices for today, even though he was moving into his forties, that eventually, he would taste the fruits of his labor. And it worked. Every time he made a profit, his first priority was to put it back into his business. He chose to use the few dollars he acquired and turn it into a positive investment for the future.

When we get that tax refund, an unexpected windfall, or a raise on our job we think, "Oh, that's not enough to do anything." We minimize the potential of a few dollars. We have all heard the stories of a church pastor who handed out a hundred one dollar bills in his service. He would tell his congregation to each take their one dollar and over the next month see how God could help them multiply it. The results are varied. Yet, each instance usually resulted in a major multiplication. Elderly ladies would knit and sew. Youth would construct crafts. The creativity flowed. When they set their minds to it, profits were made, one dollar at a time.

This whole process takes a tremendous amount of patience. We want instant gratification. We want what we want, and we want it today. Credit makes that possible. Used wisely, credit is a positive thing. Yet there is something more positive about being debt free.

For years Dana had lived the American dream. Rental houses, upkeep, car payments, living in the nine-to-five rigorous routine kept him from jumping into the adventures his heart craved. But eventually he discovered the value of using what he had. By putting his small resources to work he awakened his own creativity. Each time he put his profits back into his business; there was a renewed sense of satisfaction. The excitement of working cash and carry became more exhilarating than buying new toys on credit. Month by month Dana pared his profits, taking a bit for himself, and reinvesting in his dream. Equipment costs, fixtures, transportation, office equipment, and even advertising have been provided through this system.

Eventually he saw the fruit of this new habit he developed. Today he travels to the islands for dive trips, enjoys meals out with friends, and senses the deep satisfaction in knowing he no longer punches a clock putting profit in someone else's pockets. Today, the profits are going into Dana's pockets as he continues sailing on the crystal clear waters of his dream.

31 Advertising

Rush hour traffic escalates in the early morning light as commuters push into Atlanta from the East. Dana sits quietly sipping his coffee and reading a book. Perched comfortably behind the wheel of his van he settles in for the next couple of hours as the wind from the traffic gently rocks his van.

This is free advertising. Each morning Dana would pull his old van off the four-lane and set up shop. He purchased two adjustable paint poles and secured them in concrete blocks for stability. Between the poles was a giant red dive flag and his business information. The flag covered his van hiding it from view. Each morning he would settle in with his coffee and start his business day with a bit of advertising.

After a few days he would move to a new location and settle in again. Hundreds of drivers leaving the Conyers area saw his sign each morning. Dana said all they usually saw was the dive symbol and his phone number. But that was all it took to make his presence known.

This kind of creativity is what inspires Dana. He says, "I haven't read a lot of books on how it's supposed to be done simply because I've always been kind of creative and like to invent stuff."

32 Bring the Ocean to Them

One of Dana's idea stemmed from a fund-raiser he was involved in back in eighty-five. A group of local divers decided to raise some money for Jerry's Kids (Muscular Dystrophy). At the Double Tree Hotel on the North side of Atlanta, they set up a dive tank with windows, large enough for several divers. The objective was to play monopoly underwater, twenty-four hours a day, for a week or so. The dive shop Dana was diving with at the time was a part of the fund-raiser, so Dana and his thirteen year old daughter took their turn. As people passed by they contributed to the cause.

Dana always remembered this event and recently decided to look for his own dive tank. He would place it in strategic locations to peak people's interest in diving. He noticed one sitting in a field on the Yellow River Game Ranch, not far from his home. It had been sitting there for years collecting surface rust.

And now for the rest of the story. When Dana approached the owner he found out that it was the same tank that he and his daughter had played monopoly in for Jerry's Kids.

The owner of the Yellow River Game Ranch gave Dana the tank after he realized what he wanted to use it for. Later Dana traded advertising for the man out of gratitude. He began working on restoring and remodeling it to fit his advertising needs. He planned to set it up in various locations and demonstrate the diving process viewed through a large window. He even hoped to set up his own fundraising event.

It is these types of creative ideas which helped Dana attain his dream. Once when he entered the winter slump and few people are actually thinking of scuba diving lessons he tried a different approach. He sent a personal letter to all of his past students. It was a very informal letter, like an alumni letter, thanking them for their help in getting his business off the ground. In the letter he asks for their help in distributing a flyer offering a special discount on diver certification classes. In return for bringing in a new student they would receive 50% off on their next advanced class.   Dana tried to develop a personal loyalty in his dive family and it worked.

33 Synergy

He has discovered many forms of creative advertising which keep more cash in his pockets. Another project was to work with a local athletic club, the Covington Health and Fitness Center. He would set up a display table with textbooks, handouts, TV and a continuous running diving video. After he closed the dive shop he would set up for three hours in the foyer as people came and went. He did this two nights a week every two or three weeks. He offered a discount on dive classes to any member of that club. In return the club owner gave Dana promotional gift coupons for free visits to the club for any of Dana's dive students. There were monthly passes for those Dana felt were good prospective members for the club and day passes just for promotional purposes. Since he worked exclusively with only one club, the owner allowed him to periodically set up an information table in the entry area. Dana would display his equipment, advertise classes, and hold a drawing. The drawing was for a free certification class. One person per month would win the prize.

His display consisted of dive pictures he had found in dive magazines. Then he took the layout with the wording offering free scuba lessons to a printer friend who cleaned it up and printed color copies. He then had the posters mounted on foam display boards. He needed something to put people's registrations in so he went to a local building and supply store and bought quart paint cans with lids. He dressed up the cans with construction paper and some dive stickers. One of his students whose family owned a tool and die shop graciously cut slots in the tops of the cans. Then he glued the poster boards to the cans and placed them into golf clubs, travel areas, and other areas. His total cost was about eighty-five dollars for ten displays. This fairly inexpensive form of advertising helped Dana to draw in the needed customers for his newly developing business. These forms of advertising are not only inexpensive but are a method for interacting with people in related fields who can prove to be a valuable resource to our business in other areas.

He also hosted a monthly scuba club in his store. Every third Tuesday at 7:00 p.m. there was a special speaker. For instance, Vickie York spoke on women and diving. They also discussed a fish of the month and held a drawing. This club was a way of drawing together the alumni of Dana's classes.

There have been many creative ideas for low-cost advertising. Once he had flyers made up telling about the store and how to get there. He made his way around all the baseball and softball fields and put them on the cars. This took up a lot of time but the only cost was the flyers which were printed through barter.

34 Women in Scuba

Dana offered classes strictly for women in his newsletter and said he saw more and more women taking on the underwater adventure. "I saw women coming into the sport and bringing their families with them. That is a diving market worth pursuing."

In the teenage years of the scuba industry, back in the seventies, Dana says you very seldom saw a woman come through the door. When they did they seemed to be fit and rugged like the sky divers, and mountain climbers. Now about 30% are female students. And they are all backgrounds and interests. One of Dana's recent students was a grandmother, whereas most new divers are men between the ages of twenty-five and forty years old. Dana said he heard about one third of the new divers are women. That trend has continued to increase over the years though.

The diving manufacturers have finally taken note and begun developing lines of equipment specifically geared towards women instead of simply downsizing men's equipment. No more trying to fit into a man's suit. Underwater, men and women can enjoy the equality of the sport since they are both weightless and fifty pounds of equipment means nothing.

35 Baiting the Cruise Crowd

He also offered free snorkeling lessons to anyone signing up for a cruise with Galaxy cruises. He approached this travel agency and promised to use them exclusively. Several years later Dana teamed up with Blair Smith who was not only a dive instructor, but a travel agent. They began offering their own travel packages, but for a period in the beginning he worked with Galaxy offering students a package deal.

Most of Dana's clients, 85%, have snorkeled in clear water. He offered them free lessons with a booked cruise. The snorkeling lessons were held at the Emory College pool. He would teach a group how to snorkel and show them a video at his store location. The whole process cost him nothing. It was free advertising. He always scheduled them about thirty minutes before the scuba class ended. So they wait their turn and watch the scuba divers in the water. Then he leaves two or three sets of gear on the side of the pool to lure the snorkeling students.

He then tells them, "Before you get out, just for the fun of it why don't you try this gear on." Then they go on their Caribbean cruise and do their snorkeling thing. When they get home from their trip Dana has an ad already in their mailbox offering them scuba lessons. It worked.

He says, "Because I am a one man show I have had to come up with ways to market the business. I don't care how it's supposed to look; I just make it up and do it."

36 Careful Around the Competition

Students could find Dana in the local yellow pages but he played that form of advertising very low key.

"I wanted to be careful because some of my competition are better off financially than me and have gotten over the initial headaches. The last thing I wanted to do was alert them that I was interested in their market, as well as my own. If I heavily jumped into their area and couldn't afford to compete I would not stand in the battle with them."

Competition is something he watches closely. Once, while night diving in Catalina one of his dive buddies got a taste of the competition. Dana told me all about it.

"Catalina is a conglomerate of mountains or hills that go right down into the water. So, underneath there are a lot of jagged walls. Visibility is poor. In fact it's a little eerie. This diver was shining light on the wall in front of him at a giant lobster on the sea wall when he suddenly had the strangest feeling that he was not alone. At that point he looked over his left shoulder and saw the biggest eye he had ever seen. He screamed into the regulator and jerked, almost knocking off his mask. Right at that point, the thing brushed past his left shoulder and almost knocked his mask off. It was a Sea Lion which had its attention focused on getting the same lobster the diver was watching. "

Because the diver was shining his light on the lobster, the Sea Lion could see the same target. Before he knew what was happening, the more experienced predator grabbed the target.

That's one thing Dana tried to avoid. He was the only dive business in Rockdale County. He knew that if he spent enormous amounts on advertising, his competition could scoop up his customers. The big boys had money and resources. When Dana began his business he was on a highly restrictive budget. There was no way he could compete with his competitors. The secret was to keep his flashlight on low beam for a while, so as not to alert his competitors to a growing market opportunity.

So, Dana only advertised in the local Rockdale area yellow page ads. He watched his competitors and those who advertised their business and learned several things. Some of them would give the appearance of a thriving business, like things were happening. But many bit the dust, closing their doors before they really took off.

He also saw competitors who were making it big. Yet, every one of their customers that Dana met, seemed dissatisfied with those owners. Dana learned that these particular businesses were more concerned with high volume sales than return customers. They set up in affluent areas and draw people into their stores. Once inside they are shocked by high priced equipment, pressure sales, and add on sales. The owners have made big money, but many customers do not return. Dana has decided to go after return customers. To develop a family, an alumnus, who felt drawn back time and again.

Once, staff reporter, Barbara Knowles, of The Rockdale Citizen, a local newspaper wrote an article on Dana's business. The full page article, complete with picture, told Dana's story, presented class schedules, and gave the reader information on how to sign up.

Dana sent me the article with a note that said, "Now this is what I call an Ad!" What excited him the most was the fact that it cost him nothing. The local reporter walked in off the street and asked Dana for his story.

Through his own newsletter Dana presented timely news pieces to nearly 500 people every quarter. The eight page newsletter was a way of advertising his business but that was not his goal. His goal is to use it to make a difference in the world he lives in. That's why he has people like Dr. Delp, Blair Smith (one of his instructors), and others address safety and environmental issues. At one point he added another columnist to the paper, Rex Stutchman III, who was an environmental health specialist and dive master with PADI. One of his first articles dealt with the health hazards of traveling to exotic locales in the South Pacific. Issues like: boiling your water, avoiding ice (may not be treated) and using preventative antibiotics help cut your chances of getting the dread diarrhea.

Dana had little money for advertising and knew a newsletter could become a major expense. So, he approached a typesetter who was on trade. Remember, Dana received trade dollars from some of his students in return for certification classes. Using his trade dollars he approached Karen Winstead of Expressible Ink to set him up.

Initially she charged eighty-five dollars for the layout. After that her fee dropped to fifty dollars. He started out with only four pages, an eleven-by-seventeen sheet folded in half. Eventually, each quarter he published eight pages. The paper not only served to educate and inform his new students, but it also drew in new people with offers of unlimited diving trips to places like Ft. Lauderdale, and trips to other exotic locations.

Advertising was not one of Dana's major priorities. For one thing he tried to focus on developing a family of dive students and relied heavily on word of mouth and it worked. Even though he didn't have the major dollars required for highway billboards, slick magazine ads, or television proclamations he found ways to advertise his new business. Those things do get results, but so have Dana's methods. Scarcity of funds can be the mother of invention. Because he started with pennies, he has been forced to become creative in his advertising concepts. Actually he enjoyed coming up with new methods. Whether it's sitting by the roadside in his sign covered van, or offering snorkeling lessons to cruise clients, his methods were successful in helping him to begin his dream and finally open for business.

One of Dana's watercolors

37 Open for Business

Weightless. I hovered in the silent water neither sinking nor floating up to the surface. Surrounded by a cocoon of clear liquid I rested quietly in the womb surrounding me. I had achieved neutral buoyancy. I was weightless. The lead weights strapped around my waist allowed me to cruise smoothly through the water toward the bottom, overpowering the buoyancy of my wet suit and tank of air. As I drifted slowly toward the bottom I began pressing the air valve to release a small amount of air into my buoyancy control jacket. The jacket, a glorified life vest, was hooked to my tank and could easily be inflated when on the surface. When I descended I released all of its air. Now, close to bottom, I carefully gave it air. My descent came to a gentle halt as I began to hover quietly in the water. Still sinking a bit I added a shot of air. I leveled off and experienced the feeling of weightlessness.

Several years earlier I had been almost sixty pounds overweight. I figured it out once. That was like carrying six ten pound bags of flour around with me all the time. I balk at carrying in the groceries each week and especially try to avoid the ten pound bag of potatoes. But I was carrying around ten of those bags, on a regular basis. When I went to bed at night, there they were. When I brushed my teeth, took a shower, and got dressed, all six of them were there with me.

Over a period of four years I finally shucked that excess weight and began feeling more energy and more positive about life. But I still weighed in at close to two hundred pounds. That's a lot of weight to push against the nature of gravity. Weight is a fact of life. Something which keeps us secure to the earth. But every once in a while we enter a period when we feel free from the weight around us. For me it was underwater. When I finally achieved neutral buoyancy there was a freedom of movement. I had snorkeled many times before, drifting along the surface, peering down at the fish from a distance. Every once in a while I would take a deep breath and dive below the surface. It wasn't too difficult with my fins but there was a certain amount of effort necessary to push myself to the bottom and swim along for a minute or two. Eventually I had to bob back to the surface and rest my lungs and muscles. It wasn't very difficult but it wasn't weightlessness.

This neutral buoyancy Dana introduced me to was different. Hovering silently I could effortlessly move up, down, or sideways. Like an astronaut in a space shuttle, my slightest movement could propel me gently in any direction I chose. It was invigorating to be free from the weight of the world; to be free to just explore and enjoy my dream.

That time comes for dreamers. For years Dana had longed for the freedom to explore the world of his dreams. For years he was burdened down with the weight of the world, financial failure, divorce, and loss of his career. All he could think about was where the next check would come from to pay the bills. The weight of daily concerns, of starting a business, and of his personal struggles tried to pull him to the bottom, to sink his dream. Other priorities kept him on the surface, above the swirling waters, unable to see the beauty below.

Neutral buoyancy doesn't last forever. Eventually you have to come back to the surface, go back to work, finance your fun. But the more experienced you become, the more weightlessness you can feel. And for Dana, neutral buoyancy took time and skill development, but it did come at last.

After the remodeling on Dana's building was completed, the permits obtained, and the equipment purchased, Dana finally opened his doors. The weight of how to begin his dream was over. All those concerns and challenges that weighed him down for years were finally neutralized and on the front door hung his sign, "Ultimate Adventure Dive Center." Conyers, Georgia now knew Dana Grubbs was open for business. It was official. His cash drawer was ready. Customers came through the door and began their journey through multitudes of dive gear. Displays of masks, snorkels, and fins called them into Dana's dream. Wet suits, spear guns, and underwater lights illuminated the imaginations of these new underwater explorers.

Perched on his stool behind a display filled with knives, watches, and brochures, Dana could finally experience a sense of weightlessness. The pressures were still there, the gravity of financial pressures still pulled at him. But he had filled his store with buoyancy control devices and was now enjoying the feeling of neutral buoyancy. His store was open. Classes were scheduled in the back room. Customers were signing up, buying equipment, and preparing for an ultimate adventure of their own.

38 Benefit Package

The reality of a new business was still a struggle. There were tough times, red tape, and financial stresses. But Dana was beginning to feel the freedom from nine-to-five schedules with the airlines. His dream was coming true.

Customers turned into alumni, a family. They moved through his door into his classes, and on their way to ocean adventures. Loraine Goard one of Dana's close friends says, "I think the characteristic, long term that will make him successful is that he genuinely cares about people. He is a kind individual. People who walk through his doors become more than customers, they become friends. His goal is to become self-sufficient but his higher goal is what he can do for the people who walk through his doors." That type of customer service seems lost on many businesses today, but it is certainly a main draw for most customers.

Dana continued to help others, not only with such things as finding jobs, but with discovering new underwater adventures. Every other month there was a Crystal River trip for certification. Advanced classes traveled to Panama City for night dives and ninety-foot dives on shipwrecks. There were dives in Key West and Islands such as the Caymans.

Dana said, "As an instructor you do very few pleasure dives. Most dives you are watching students, so the Cayman trip is fun for me."

He has stayed at Coconut Harbor, fed the Stingrays by hand, and enjoyed catamaran cruises. Coconut Harbor is located one-half mile south of George Town, Grand Cayman. Dana stayed in a thirty-five room studio apartment resort overlooking the ocean and some of Cayman's most beautiful reefs. People dive day and night, right from the hotel. He remembers one of those dives.

"There was Yellowtail everywhere. As we descended down the anchor line there was a gentleman and his wife just above me. She was having a little trouble equalizing pressure and he was carrying food in his pockets to feed the fish. It was dissolving and filtering down towards me. Yellowtails were everywhere, all around me like flies. They don't have teeth but one pecked at my ear. I think he thought my earlobe was food. They pecked at my knee, the tip of my fins, and I just kept shooing them away like flies."

During that trip he was also able to dive on a wreck called the Overta which was eventually torn up by hurricanes and high seas. Each year Dana tried to plan a trip to the Caymans with friends and a few advanced students. That's the feeling he had longed for, to be free for diving adventures. It has been an exhilarating experience for him, to be free from the weight of mundane repetitive activity, and to be able to travel to the depths of new waters.

In the Olympic summer when people were thinking of the summer games in Atlanta, Dana was already planning another Cayman Island trip. "The trip is starting to fill up," he reported in his newsletter," and it was only July. He wondered what was going on. Could the word be out? The trip was in February 1997 and there were already five signed up and that was not counting himself and Blair (one of his instructors). He said, "We would be doing some advance check-outs as well as many specialties ratings." He remembered that the previous February the Caymans were trapped in the grip of a cold wave. The temperature was only eighty-two degrees which was cool for that area. Yet, that did not deter this new team that was already signing up.

Dana's business was beginning to grow. The weight of the world was still there, but the feeling of neutral buoyancy was exhilarating as he began more programs and drew in more students. In June of 1996 Dana took his program out the Bert Adams Boy Scout camp to introduce scuba to some boys who may never have had the chance for such an adventure.

He said, "Its times like these that make scuba so special!" For Dana, these times are what he dreamed of. Through the times of swirling confusion he knew someday, these days would come. Diving is an adventure; for him - the ultimate adventure.

In an interview by the local "Rockdale Citizen" newspaper Dana was quoted as saying, "It's something that most divers will tell you is hard to explain in words. You get out and get away and when you're underwater and are actually breathing on scuba, it's impossible to think about anything else. If you have a high stress job, it's instant relaxation."

He recalled on a trip to the Cayman Islands how he taught one of his students how to get an "underwater manicure.

"There are places underwater called cleaning stations where a fish will actually swim up to. It's like a car wash," he explained. "Little tiny fish and Cleaner Shrimp about an inch long will come out and attach themselves to the fish and clean parasites off them. The fish will stay there until he's clean and then he'll swim away. You can lay your hands down there and be real still and the shrimp will come out and feel the end of your fingers and then crawl up on your fingers and actually eat the dead skin from around your fingernails."

39 Dreams Became Reality

It was just these types of experiences, sharing these times with his students and friends that Dana dreamed of. And finally it became a reality. The days of nine to five, punching in and punching out were a distant dream. His Eastern Airline days had faded into the past. Yet, he still hoped to somehow reach his fellow employees, and those suffering from downsizing America with his example. He is proud of the fact that he started his shop on a shoe string, taking it slow and easy, and could finally make a living doing what he loved the most.

In the news article Dana said that a couple of years ago, he looked into the demographics of that area and although it was not exactly perfect for a dive shop, he knew in another five years it would be. That would give him time to build up his clientele and that's exactly what he did. He was the only dive shop in the Rockdale area. The closest competitor he had was about 35-40 minutes away by car.

Dana finally opened the doors of his dive shop. It took time to work through the financial details, collect his stock and furnishings, and advertise his new business. But, it paid off. Back in the Airline days, when he walked the picket lines week after week, his dream felt impossible. He worked through the "deep-pockets" thinking. He worked through the struggles of finding a location and getting the dealers to listen to him. But he did it, one step at a time.

Slowly, and patiently he worked his dream. He could have continued dreaming for another ten years. Instead he swam one lap - one at a time. He collected his stores, found ways to trade business and supplies, and finally opened his doors.

Dana knows the downsizing effect on American minds and even more so in our current economic state. He knows the discouragement and frustration. He knows what it is like to lay in bed at night and wish he could make a change. It is his hope that those who are still struggling to make a living will one day find the will to do as he has done. The treasures below the surface are still there.

Treasure ships like the Atoche are still giving up its treasures and there is more to come. The oceans are full of wealth and adventure for those who are willing to take the plunge, to take the risk. Taking a risk fills many people with trepidation and fear. How can I invest what I don't have? What difference can this pocket change make? Where would I ever find the resources to start to pursue my own dream? These kinds of questions keep many of us swirling in whirlpools of confusion.

America has been labeled the land of opportunity. Many don't believe it anymore. "The fifties are gone", they say. "The days of opportunity are past." Yet year after year, immigrants continue to travel to our shores and from meager beginnings build their dream. How can they do it? Granted, some have the resources when they come to America. But others come in poverty. What is their secret? They still believe. They believe that a person who works hard, is patient, and takes a risk, can still find the American dream.

The dream seems impossible at times. We tend to look at other people who are currently successful and ascertain in our minds that we can't do it. We look at the businessman with a chain of stores, the consultant with a multiple staff, or the flourishing franchise and feel weighted down with their success. Rather than seeing that first step that they took, we focus on the finished product. We don't see those first few weeks and years of starting on a shoe-string. It is easy to become overwhelmed by the big picture, to look at someone like Dana Grubbs, settled into a growing business, and feel a sense of overpowering magnitude.

It is important to keep our perspective. We can focus on the choppy waters above the surface and never descend below the surface. We must remember that it takes one lap at a time.

The weight of negative thinking holds many people on the bottom. Unable to move or function, they robotically continue their drudgery, sloshing around in debt and frustration. But Dana Grubbs is one of those pioneers who grasped the silly idea that it is still possible to find a dream. He knows it can be done. He did it and continues to do it. And he is convinced that you can do it too.

40 Picking up Momentum

"The Ultimate Adventure Dive Center, invites you to attend our CAYMAN MADNESS PARTY. That's right, we're headed back and we want to take you with us."

It is a hot Georgia night, a bit muggy, the sound of crickets in the air as I pull up to the countryside home of one of Dana's friends. I expect a little get together in someone's family room, some homemade pizza, and a short canned talk about the adventures of diving.

The lush thick manicured lawn surrounds the large two-story house. I follow others up the long driveway to the cedar gate out back.

I step into Jamaican music dancing across a large fenced in backyard. Curved topped cedar fence surrounds a huge wrap around deck which steps down onto a concrete patio area surrounding a blue-bottom lighted swimming pool. In its center a fountain undulates gently between two red diver's flags at each end of the pool.

Etched grass rims the edges of the patio leading up to a white gazebo filled with guitars and sound equipment. A half dozen Tiki torches stood flickering along the fence line. White wrought iron tables and chairs are already filled with anxious divers, diver wanna-bes, and their families.

Up front a four-foot by eight-foot banner with large red letters announces, "Now in Conyers, Ultimate Adventure Dive Center."

As I step into the festive atmosphere I am greeted by Lynne Browning sitting at a guest registration table. Recently Lynne had begun working with Dana, helping run the store freeing him up for the dive trips and other store business. She fills out my name tag and puts my name in a pot for a drawing later. A dive skin (wet suit) and a dive equipment bag will be given away.

I walk past the four-foot by eight-foot red dive flag hanging between the windows on a large red brick fireplace on the outside wall. Along the wall on the deck are tables loaded with shrimp, chicken wings, shish kabobs of scallops and shrimp, and a feast of other delights.

I spot Lorraine Gourd, Dana's friend from Tradebank, at the grill basting kabobs, coolers full of them. People are everywhere. There are young college students, some of Dana's buddies from Eastern Airlines, families, and single people. Two little girls in red dresses twirl near the pool in time with the island music permeating the night air. Groups of people huddle around picture displays of past Cayman trips, reminiscing about the good times they had or the ones they expected on their next trip.

Suddenly someone is taping the microphone up front in the gazebo. Dana, wearing blue knee length shorts, white socks, black tennis shoes, a yellow polo shirt, and a straw hat with a maroon band, welcomes his family. They applaud and the party begins.

Throughout the long night, door prizes are given, stories shared, and music is listened to. At one point someone requested that Dana sing an oldie, The Wreck of The Edmond Fitzgerald. Several people moan, but I settle into the thick green grass with my plate of shrimp and experienced one of Dana's many talents. In the old days he would occasionally bring in some cash playing in local restaurants. Now he uses his guitar and voice to entertain his friends and students. He is not a seasoned professional but is actually very good. One of his friend's jumps in and Dana accompanies while he croons out something about, "wasting away again in Margaretville."

Dana is pleased. Thirty people have signed up for the February trip, and it is only 9:00 pm on a hot August night. That gives Dana three free trips, one for each ten people. That meant one for himself, one for Blair Smith (one of his instructors), and now one for a friend who sponsored the party. As usual Dana has worked a deal on the party. His friend would get a free trip, and would open up his home, provide some food and drinks, and help clean up the mess afterwards. Dana was able to get some of the food and the advertising on trade.

Standing up front, Dana announces the breakdown of trip costs for those who still haven't made a decision. Thirteen hundred dollars covered: air fare, one week in the hotel, continental breakfast, unlimited boat and shore dives (available 24 hours a day), a visit to sting ray city, and a cruise on a racing catamaran.

The evening is a culmination of Dana's years of dreaming. He is doing what he loves the most and now it was a time to celebrate. His old buddies from Eastern Airlines and others eat and drink in celebration of their friend's success.

At 10:30 Dana tells me he wants to say goodbye to a couple leaving the party. As he walks toward the pool a scene reminiscent of a Mafia hit unfolds before me. I am as shocked as Dana would be. Three men suddenly emerge from the crowd of people and step quickly into Dana's path. Before he comprehends the seriousness of that moment he is hoisted into the air in a dramatic arc over the pool by his friends. As he sputters to the surface and his straw hat floats off toward the flowing fountain, they cheer.

The party is primed. Two more divers end up in the pool. The fountain wavers erratically in the center. A man with the build of a bear is grabbed by two women and one man. Their attempt to drag him into the pool is pathetic. They give up. The big man looks for his prey.

The Sam Davis family sits on lounge chairs next to me. The big man came with them, a friend of theirs. Sam runs a large automotive repair facility and met Dana through trade. He has treated his whole family to dive certification and trips. Sam's teenage daughter is suddenly scooped up by the big man. She is tossed like a toy into the pool. She doesn't mind, she wanted to swim anyway she says.

Dana comes over and sits next to me. As we talk about the fact that Dana tried to invite two reps from the Cayman resort to this party, the big man throws in the Davis girl again.

"Someone needs to do something," I tell Dana. He agrees. Suddenly I am beside myself, a moment of temporary insanity. I step quickly and quietly toward the pool. He doesn't see me. I give one massive push. Nothing happens. Before he turns around, I give one last effort. He is in. Everyone cheers. Five minutes later he is conversing with me about something, never realizing I was his perpetrator.

Two more guys jump in the pool. A guitarist is plunking out some tune in the gazebo, and the music still pumps out from the speakers on the back of the house. More kabob is grilled, drinks poured, and shrimp skewered. Everyone is laughing – dreaming - anticipating their trip to the Caymans. Two girls run in fear from pool thugs. They hide in the house. They are safe.

Dana tells the crowd that the resort has thirty-two rooms. So far they have twenty reserved. There is applause. Dana tells me he will make a considerable profit for his store on this trip so far. He will also make profit on dive equipment he sells for the trip. He will sell at least ten sets of gear.

With the excitement of a political convention Dana tells everyone that someone else has just signed up. There is more applause. There is even a girl who they may certify on the trip itself. This is met with the enthusiasm of a couple announcing their engagement, which also happens. Dianne was in my certification class. Her dream is to become an instructor. On her certification trip to Crystal River, she met her fiancée. They are getting married. I asked if the ceremony would be under water. Dianne laughs and says they are considering it. But they are going for a honeymoon in a hotel in Florida. They have heard that it is only accessible by scuba diving into it.

Dana has not only ushered them into the world of diving, but has been the vehicle which transported them into a new life. I think that Dana should do the wedding, but that's not his job. His job, his dream is to live an adventure.

And on this hot Georgia night in deep August, Dana Grubbs is watching things heat up. The flow is rapidly increasing. He whispers to me that his profits have increased dramatically over the past year. I go for another serving of shrimp. It is midnight, the dawn of a new day, and the party is still building anticipation.

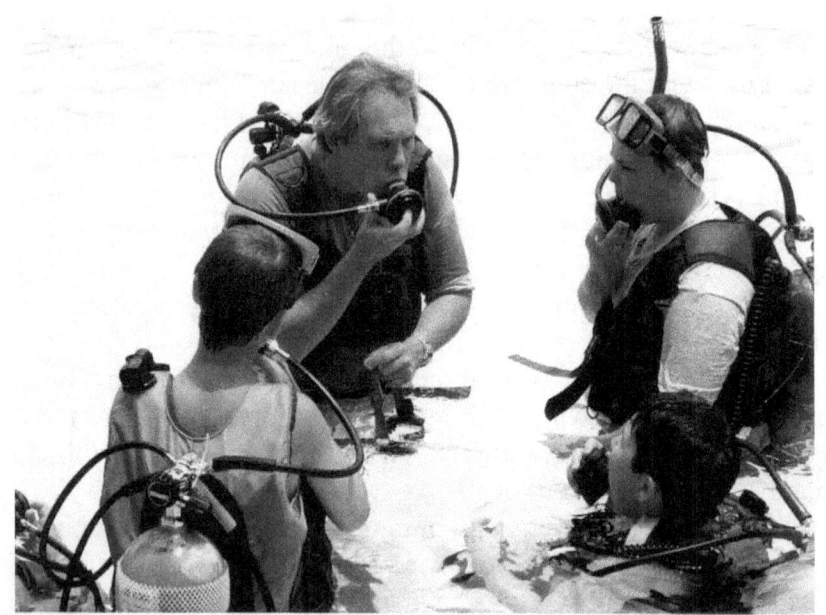

41 Islamadora

"This dive in the Florida Keys turned out to be the dive of the trip. I personally would not want to repeat it," Dana tells me. After anchoring the wind had let up but the sky was still dark to the west of us. Lane Britt, the owner of a dive shop in south of Atlanta, and a good friend of mine, was leading the way because he was good with the compass. He and I went in and started our movement around the reef. Little did I know the current was gradually pushing us farther and farther from the boat.

After some time, exploring the reef, I started getting low on air so I got Lanes attention and he started leading back to the anchor line. But with the cross current we had both gotten turned around.

After searching for a while, and using up more air, we finally decided to surface and see where we were. When we broke the surface the waves were around four and a half feet and the boat looked to be about one hundred yards away.

When he saw the situation all Lane could say was, 'Ho! Shit!' The storm was on us and we knew we would have to swim like hell to get back to the boat. I started swimming toward the bow in hopes of hitting the stern. The current was running strong on the surface.

As I started to swim I looked down at my pressure gauge and saw it registered only eight hundred psi (pounds per square inch). As I swam through the waves my heart was pounding and my breathing rate had become rapid. I don't know if it was the panic or the fact that I was swimming so hard.

After swimming hard for a minute or so I realized I'd have to slow down and get control of my breathing, because my psi had dropped to five hundred and if I couldn't breathe through my regulator I'd quickly drown.

At three hundred psi I seemed a little closer and I could see other divers at the rear of the boat. The rain started falling so hard I could feel it hitting the top of my head even with the wave action.

Down to one hundred psi I finally reached the drift line but other divers were blocking my way. So, I moved to the other side of the platform. Just as I grabbed the metal platform I took my last breath from my tank. It was empty."

The drive of Dana's business was picking up momentum. There were trips and Cayman madness parties, yet occasionally there were still those dark days when storm clouds moved over the horizon and he felt like giving it all up.

There were times when Dana considered giving up his diving dream. Times when he was down to his last breath. Times when he poured over the bills and receipts and wondered if it was all worth the struggle, fighting against the currents, swimming in high seas. Discouragement was not a stranger in his business. The winter lulls were at times overwhelming. Few customers chose to embark on an adventure in the cool southern days. He would sit for hours, alone in his store, waiting for just one customer to come in through the front door.

There were times when he thought back to the security of the nine-to-five routines. Solid paychecks and freedom from the fear of failure haunted him. Discouragement crept in as he tried desperately to fight his way through the storms and conserve his air as long as possible.

42 Facing Fears

Another Islamorada diver met with tragic results. In September of 1996 a scuba diver named William Covert of Michigan faced his own personal tragedy. Authorities aren't sure if he was killed by a twelve foot bull shark or if he ran out of air, drowned, and was later eaten by the shark. All that was found was bits of his diving gear, an empty tank, and a weight belt. There were teeth marks on the suit, but none on the belt. Covert evidently had run out of air on previous dives, unbuckled his weight belt, dropped his tank, and swam for the surface. Either way, it appeared that he had been attacked by the shark at some point.

It was reported that in 1996 shark attacks were increasing dramatically with the state of Florida leading the statistics. Since 1990 the reported bites in Florida had reached eighty-eight as opposed to the one hundred and seventy-nine worldwide. According to the International Shark Attack File, Florida had more attacks that year than the past five years – a dramatic increase.

But, there is more to this story. A person could read these statistics, hear about a diver losing his life, and decide never to visit Islamorada, Florida, or any other dive spot in the world. The truth is that Florida has seen a dramatic increase in surfing and swimming activities over the past years. And reports show that most shark attacks are not really attacks but merely bites by small sharks that get confused in turbid waters and think they were going after another fish. Many shark stories are pushed passionately out of proportion. In fact, most divers never meet up with dangerous specie of shark and when they do there is usually no danger, just simple observation. Most species encountered are: grays, sand tigers, bulls, nurses, and on rare occasions, a hammerhead. The rare Great Whites are normally found off the coast of Australia or in a few areas around Northern California. These are rarely encountered by any recreational diver.

Dana told me that many documentaries where you see hordes of sharks looming around dive cages, voraciously attacking raw meat, have actually been chummed for days in advance by the set-up crews to insure there would indeed be sharks present for the filming.

No doubt, sharks are dangerous. There have been many tragic experiences. Yet, the shark attack is highly overrated. Yes, the diver must respect the shark, and be very wary when intruding into their domain. But too many people have heard the horror stories about shark attacks and vow never to venture into the underworld adventures. When Dana almost ran out of air at Islamorada, he could have given up diving for good, afraid that someday he might drown.

Shark attacks and drowning are realities that must be taken seriously. We all have our Islamorada, a place or event or fear which tempts us to run away from our adventures. The dangers are a reality. Yet, there is danger in any endeavor. There is danger in beginning our new business, breaking out on our own, or pressing ahead into our dream. We might go under. We may sink. But we may also survive, and swim in new waters.

Diving into the waters of Islamorada was an exciting adventure for Dana. Diving into his dream was a greater adventure. Yet, despite the possible dangers lurking in the depths, he never gave up on the journey.

43 Search and Rescue

The four new graduates of Dana's Search and Rescue class stood on the shore against the rocks, smiling as their picture was taken. Excitement was high. They had just completed their classroom training, pool sessions, and finally this certification process complete with role playing exercises.

Suddenly, from about two hundred yards out in the lake, there was a cry for help. No one seemed to hear it except Dana, his instructors, and myself. The new recruits were too caught up in their celebration. There was another cry as I watched the diver slip below the surface.

Dana and I waited patiently, not making a move. One of the recruits finally asked if anyone had heard that. One of the others said they thought they heard someone too.

"This is a joke, right?" one of them asked.

"Yes, it is" one of the instructors advised, but it is part of the test."

Finally, after two or three minutes the recruits scrambled for their dive gear, jumping into the procedures they had just integrated. One stood on the rocks and directed another diver to go to the spot where the supposed drowning victim had submerged. Luckily there were bubbles. The other divers helped each other with their equipment as they raced for the water. Within a few minutes they had surfaced with their victim and had him floating on his back with the help of his buoyancy control jacket. As they maneuvered him towards the shore I could hear the counting between breaths as they administered CPR.

"One-thousand one, one-thousand two, one-thousand three, one-thousand four, breathe." Between breaths they would unstrap pieces of equipment such as the weight belt, mask and snorkel, and as they neared the shoreline, the buoyancy control jacket. In two foot of water one of the rescuers attempted to sling the body over his shoulders, fireman style. But, they both fell into the sand rolling in laughter.

"This is how it always happens," Dana said, referring to this last exercise. "I put one of my instructors in the water, everyone has already started packing up their equipment, and when they hear the cry for help, they think it's a joke."

Dana went on to explain how that is exactly what happens many times when divers hear an actual cry for help. They don't believe it. They wonder if it's for real. The shock of reality takes a moment to sink in before the adrenaline kicks in and they hit the water.

The same principle applies when we begin to see success in beginning our dream. The struggle is long and hard. We put in our classroom time, our pool sessions, and our exercises. It was tough but we got through it. We become so exhilarated with the success in front of us that it feels intoxicating. Let the party begin! We begin to think that we have made it. One sweet success, one major sale, one good weekend, and we suddenly think the race is over. It's not over. It is just beginning. Now, everything we have learned comes to the forefront. Just when we think we have it made, there is an unexpected challenge in front of us. More government fees, a slowing business season, or rising manufacturers' costs suddenly grasp our attention again. As we stand on shore we are shocked to realize something is sinking beneath the waves. At first we wonder if it is true, is it really happening. After the shock passes, we need to jump into action and find an immediate way to begin the search for solutions or a way to rescue our failing resources.

It would be easy to sit back in frustration and decide it's just too much. Many people are faced with these same situations. Dana has been through many of them. Just as his business began to take off and he began experiencing some success, business slowed for the season. He could have given up. He felt like it at times. Instead he continued to press ahead, one lap at a time.

That day with his search and rescue class they returned to the water after lunch for more of the same fun, pulling the victims up from the bottom, taking their gear off and then their own, giving mouth-to-mouth, then bringing the mock victim out of the water. Over and over again Dana's team repeated the exercises until everyone was ready to drop. And then they would do it one more time.

44 Teamwork is a Must

Marissa Wagner Moran shared a little known fact with me. "There was a treasure ship called a Karak that traveled alone so that if it sank, no one would live to tell about it. If someone found this, it would be the most impressive treasure ship find ever. That's why most treasure ships traveled in groups of at least three, so if one went down, the others could salvage the victim or at least know where it went down."

When Dana trained his rescue teams he emphasized the need to work together. One helped the other put on equipment. They race out together. Each had their own task to perform. Teamwork is an absolute necessity. Obviously there are times when the rescue is a one man operation. You need to go with what you have. But it is best to form a team. If your dream is to begin an urban arts center, one of your first steps should be to develop a team, a board, or whatever you want to call it. Someone needs to be responsible for accounting; another person needs to be the public relations person, etc. Everyone needs to have their expertise. The team works together. That way when the crisis comes, you are not running into the waves alone. Each team member jumps in together.

Maybe all you want to do is start a freelance writing business, with no desire for a corporate structure. Writing can be a very isolating endeavor. Even writers need encouragement. I know writers who have begun to utilize the online Internet services. They have become part of online writers groups, chat rooms, and bulletin boards. The writer can get into a group discussion or simply go into a chat room and vent his frustrations. Isolation can drown a writer or anyone else who tries to go it alone. The team can work together to rescue the dream from destruction. When home business owners are asked what they really miss about their corporate careers about one third say socializing and many say they miss being part of a team. Whether you are starting a home business or a major corporation, it is important to build a solid foundation you can count on for survival in the storms.

Dana knows this principle well. His friends from the airline days, people like Loraine Goard, and his family of students all serve to support him in the tough times. There have been days when he swallowed too much water or felt like he was out of air. The temptation was to just give it up. For a while he felt like he was like a drowning victim. But as he stepped back from the problems, searched for a solution, and turned to his team for support, there was a miraculous rescue of his dream.

45 Waking up to Reality

Many of us are perfectionists when it comes to formulating a plan for our dream. Our dream feels like something we will never attain. That's part of the magic. A dream is not mundane everyday living. It is something that excites us, something which builds our excitement and hope. When we think about our dream we imagine great things. Our dream is a dream. In other words, it's just a little bit distant, out of focus, and is slathered in expectation.

The problem is most of us wake up. At least that is what we call it - waking up to reality. We look out across the sunlit sea and suddenly hear the voice of our spouse telling us to take out the trash or our boss telling us to get a report out in ten minutes. Suddenly, our dream is shattered. The reality of zero finances, not knowing how to do it, and the time commitment creep over our sunlit sea like a gale blowing a ship off course. Our dream turns into a nightmare; a frustrating nightmare that makes us feel hopeless.

Waking up to reality, holds many people right where they are. I was with someone recently and told her about Dana's concept of going after a dream. She laughed and said it was a nice thought, but the reality is that most people can't do it. I asked why not. Methodically, she explained such reasons as: lack of money, lack of time, and lack of opportunity. As we talked further I realized that each of these roadblocks could be overcome with Dana's principles. A couple of meals out might buy a piece of used office equipment. It may take time, yet the question remains, what will you will be doing five years from now if you don't follow your dream. There may not be an opportunity which offers quick, easy, access, but most opportunities are birthed by a dreamer.

What we label "reality" is many times no more than our own psychological limitations. We perceive various roadblocks as permanent structures. When my wife and I look at a prospective house for investment I will go for the fixer-uppers. All she sees is lack of closet space, tiny rooms, and peeling plaster. I'm usually the visionary in our family and see something else. I see a wall between two small rooms. Yes, it is a wall, but I also see myself busting out that wall and creating - voila! - a family room. I see peeling plaster, but I also see myself stripping the walls and recovering them with new drywall and fresh smelling paint. I can even visualize a new deck off our bedroom with a sauna in a small greenhouse.

It would be easy for us to glance at a house and abruptly pass it off as a lost cause. Too many of us treat our dreams the same way. Briefly, we see a cozy cottage in our mind, the one we've always wanted, the one on the lake. Then we shake our head and get back to "reality". We tell ourselves it will never happen, not enough money, not enough time, and soon our dream fades into the night. The difficulty for many people is in using what they have and building from there.

Dana Grubbs had several dive trips and a dream of being his own boss. He had no money, he was getting up towards his forties, and he didn't have the slightest idea how to proceed. It would not have been difficult for him to look at his dive dream and say it was just too much. He could have accepted his fate of failure and let others do it. Instead he decided to go with what he had and that wasn't much.

What some people call reality is actually illusion. They assume they can do nothing when the reality is they could do much. They say the reality is that they have no money, so their assumption is that the task is impossible. That is an illusion. The reality is that there are numerous resources and options all around us if we just study and search for them.

Dana is one of those people. He knew the risks. He understood the barriers, at least some of them. Yes he did encounter red tape, outrageous building codes, and slow sales. Yet, he was willing to start with what he had. It wasn't much - few vacation days, a PADI instructor course, and the commitment to press on through the storm.

As a young boy watching the weekly adventures of "Sea Hunt" on television, and he dreamed. He may not have had much to work with, but he had a dream. Year after year he took step after step. Reality became distorted at times with the voices who said it couldn't be done. He never gave up on his dream.

46 Focusing on the Right Cause

The icy rain blew hard against my van as I picked up my daughters Wendy, and Megin, and Wendy's friend Rachel. It was Friday afternoon in Atlanta, mid-February, and we were in the midst of record cold spell.

"Still wanna go?" I asked as they climbed in.

A resounding "yes!" was their response, so we plodded on through a rain slicked highway 75 toward Crystal River, Florida. By the time we reached our destination the weather had raised to a sunny sixty degree day. Wendy and Rachel decided to go shopping and hit the tanning salon. They didn't want their friends back home to know the Florida beaches were unbearable, lashed with briskly cold breezes, so they opted for artificial burns.

They dropped Megin and me off at the Best Western where Dana and his new dive recruits were about to head out for their diver certification dive. At eight a.m. the next morning we met in the dive shop to gear up. The staff fit us with wet suits and we loaded our equipment onto the pontoon. But first we were required to watch the Manatee awareness video. That's what we had come for, to see these mammals first hand. The video informed us of an endangered species, delicate, gentle, which needed special protection by government agencies. Our group watched in excited anticipation as the narrator instructed us to stay out of roped off areas used as havens for the Manatees. Our excited group finally boarded the pontoon and headed for King Spring, one of the hot spots for viewing Manatees.

On our leisurely trip out we donned our wet suits and checked our regulators. Occasionally, we passed a Manatee sign which warned motor craft to keep speeds below fifteen miles per hour and steer clear of the Manatees. For years, happy-go-lucky enthusiasts had raced through the spring fed river clipping the backs of these slow moving mammals with boat propellers. Finally, the environmental agencies clamped down and took steps to protect this endangered species.

The river, spring fed, emptied into the Gulf of Mexico just north of Tampa. Its constant seventy-two degree waters were a winter haven for the Manatee. February was an ideal time for spotting them. Later in the spring they headed back into ocean waters. On this day, despite the sunshine, most of us were shivering by the time we reached the spring. As Dana gave his class final instructions, he told me I could go ahead and get in the water since I was already certified from my last trip.

A twinge of trepidation suddenly flowed over me. On my last trip I only saw one Manatee -- briefly. Now their numbers had increased dramatically. I found myself wondering if I really wanted to jump in alone. What would I encounter? Dana noticed I was taking my time and said, "I thought you'd be in the water by now."

Shivering from the cold air I finally stepped off the edge in full scuba gear. Holding my mask tight against my face I plunged into the eight foot deep water. I bobbed to the surface yelling to the others, "It's warm! It's like a hot tub in here."

The seventy-two degree water immediately put an end to my shivering and I began peering below the surface. The water was clear and I could see the silty bottom below. No Manatees. I began to relax. Then my daughter Megin jumped in wearing only a wet suit. She was fourteen years old and this was her first time using a mask, snorkel, and fins. Since she was not yet a diver, she would just be snorkeling. I gave her some quick lessons and we swam together, heading over to the spring.

Dana stayed behind preparing his students for the adventure ahead. There were dozens of Manatee in the water that day, exactly what he had hoped for. This was part of Dana's dream. He not only wanted to open the doors of this new world, but he also had a higher vision. Early on, Dana knew he wanted to do more than make money; he wanted to tap into a cause that would widen the vision of his students.

47 The Right Cause

It began when he stepped out to begin his own training. Dana had been given that assignment in map making during his PADI training in California. All he had to do was work up a map of the area but his artistic background prompted him to embellish. He added the whale.

From those early days the whale became a symbol of something mysterious, something greater than the dive experience. When Dana finally saw his dream developing he couldn't forget that experience. He knew that the dive business was his dream. He knew that he wanted to open the doors for the adventurer's heart to see and feel the wonders of the ocean world. But he also felt he needed a higher purpose, something to focus on that was greater than the business, a vision greater than simply diving.

That's when he came up with the idea of environmental issues. There had to be something more significant than just teaching people to have fun. He wanted to instill a higher cause in their hearts and grasp something for himself which would make an impact on his world.

The manatees of Crystal River, and the Right Whales off the Georgia coastline became two of Dana's pet projects. Every year the whales migrate up the coast of Georgia to spawn. No one is sure where they go the rest of the year but each year these mysterious creatures make their way to Dana's home coast of Georgia. The fact that they are one of the most endangered species in the world intrigued Dana. The Right Whale became a focus of Dana's dream. He decided that his divers needed to be educated patrons of the undersea world, protectors of their haven.

Dana learned that the Right Whale earned its name from early whalers. When it was hunted and finally harpooned, these mammoth creatures would float on the surface making the whaler's job easy pickings. The one that floated after the slaughter was the Right Whale, the one to go after. That reputation earned these creatures the current standing as a highly endangered species. Some estimates indicate that no more that 300-325 survive in North Atlantic waters today. They can grow to about fifty feet and sixty tons. They weigh between 90,000 and 100,000 pounds and are characterized by this huge size and their slow pace. It is their high percentage of blubber (body fat) which causes them to float after death and which provided oil products for the marketplace. They also have a tendency to swim near the coast and are easily identifiable by their "blow" (the explosive burst of air exhaled by the whale on surfacing). Approximately every three years they bear young with a twelve-to-eighteen month gestation period. Calves nurse for another twelve months before weaning. They submerge anywhere from a few minutes to an hour. From May to November, they are found in northern waters (near Massachusetts, Maine, Nova Scotia and Canada) feeding and breeding. Between November and March, mother Right Whales travel to the waters off Georgia and northern Florida to give birth. No one knows where the other Right Whales go between November and May.

It seems like an impossibility to lose just one fifty-ton whale, yet each winter the whereabouts of approximately 250 whales becomes a mystery. In 1984 teams from the New England Aquarium, scientists and volunteer pilots from the Ocean Society discovered that most pregnant Right Whales travel in the winter to coastal Georgia and northern Florida waters. Despite complete international protection from hunting since 1937, this species has failed to show any signs of population recovery. Environmental groups across the world have taken up the cause. Dana decided to do his part.

Dana worked with a program to adopt a Right Whale by going into schools and educating children about this endangered species. For thirty-five dollars, a class could adopt a whale, get a photo of it, receive updates on where it was last sighted, and get a diploma showing the class name. The Ocean Society had developed the adopt a whale program even giving names to each whale like: Symmetry, Mono, Crimp, and Rat. A short history is given for each one. For instance Symmetry was born in 1993 and has been tracked as a calf to the age of reproduction. She had her first calf at the age of nine. It is noted that right whales can live up to seventy years. Detailed information is given about the whale a person adopts. They are provided with such information as: updates of whale research, a biography of your whale and its sighting history, scientific illustrations of the right whales, a summary of their biology and current status, a composite drawing of the whale showing all features used to identify it, tax deduction information, a large color photograph of the whale, and a certificate of sponsorship.

Dana's goal was to become more than a financial endeavor putting money in his own pockets. Dana said his goal became, "...first to change people's lives and make the environment a better place to live. I would do that to the best of my ability. My second priority would be the retail and financial end. So far, I've been true to my goal."

48 A Forum for His Issues

The Right Whale isn't Dana's only concern. There are others. When he began publishing his own newsletter for the dive shop he approached environmental engineer (and diver), Glen Grossman, Dana asked him to write an occasional column. Glen held a post with the Sierra Club. He gave Glen free reign to write about anything, timberland, lakes, and any environmental issue.

It was at that time that Dana also asked Doctor Delk who specializes in diving issues, to write his quarterly column. His specialty was in the area of medicine (stings, puncture wounds, etc.). As a dive master, Doctor Delk understood the possible hazards of the dive industry.

Dana handled the front page of his newsletter and usually focused on the key environmental issues in educating his divers. The Right Whale was only one of those key issues. He also offered opportunities to get involved in river clean-up projects and Appalachian Trail Club opportunities. The Appalachian Trail Club has chapters up and down the trail assigned to help keep markers in place and maintain the trails attractiveness. From Dana's home state of Georgia (the trails beginning point), all the way to Maine, the members planted flowers, cleaned up, and helped preserve the natural environment.

One day Dana hoped to take a summer off from his business and hike the trail himself which he eventually did. In the meantime he continued educating others to the needs of creatures such as the Manatees needing our protection. Blair Smith, one of Dana's instructors who helps with the checkout dives to Crystal River said, "The feeling you get after seeing a Manatee for the twentieth time is the same excitement as seeing one for the first time."

In one of his newsletter articles Dana prepared his students with, "So you're headed to Crystal River to dive with the world famous Manatees? Let's take a few minutes before you dive into their home to get to know a little about the Manatee. The Manatees we see in Crystal River are West Indian manatee. Three other living species of manatee exist. These three species are the West African manatee, the Amazonian manatee, and the Dugong. A fifth species existed; however, the Stellar's Seacow was hunted to extinction in 1741. The West Indian manatee has two subspecies. These subspecies are the Florida manatee and the Antillean manatee. Obviously, we will be diving with the Florida manatee. The Florida Manatee makes its summer home in waters as far west as Louisiana and as far north as Virginia and the Carolinas. When temperatures fall, the manatees seek the warmer waters provided by Florida's springs. The average adult male manatee is ten feet long and weighs 1200 pounds. (Don't forget that he's going to appear 25% larger and closer underwater). Manatees can grow to a length as great as thirteen feet and 3000 pounds. Female manatees reach sexual maturity at about age seven. They only give birth to one calf every two to five years. The manatee's gestation period is thirteen months. Newborn manatee calves are four to five feet long and weigh about seventy pounds. The calves nurse underwater for three minutes at a time from nipples located underneath the mother's flippers. Manatees are herbivores. They eat a variety of marine plants. The manatee consumes about sixty to one hundred pounds of food per day. Listen carefully near the manatee. You can actually hear the manatee chewing."

The article continued with, "A word about manatee etiquette and the laws that protect the manatee. The manatee is protected by the Federal Marine Mammal Protection Act of 1972 and the Endangered Species Act of 1973 at a federal level. Florida also has state and local legislation to protect the manatee. Portions of Crystal River are designated sanctuary areas. (We'll show you where the sanctuary begins and ends). You may not approach the manatee. They will come to you if they want their belly rubbed. We also cannot feed the manatee. The best tactic for interacting with the manatee is slow, quiet movement. They see a lot of divers every day. If they are in the mood they'll come to see you. NEVER pursue or chase a manatee. The waters of Crystal River are heavily patrolled and the rangers are authorized to issue steep fines. Although it seems like an awful lot that we can't do when diving with the manatee, please remember we are in their home. Currently, the population of Florida is at approximately 2000 manatee. The human population of Florida increases by approximately 2000 every three days. With these people come additional threats to the manatee's habitat. More boats come with more people; as does declining water quality, increased riverbank development and destruction of the sea grasses on which the manatee graze."

The manatees literally became hands on experience for Dana's students. He said, "I wondered how I could put people in touch with one of these species. I figured that since we do our certification at Crystal River that seemed like a natural place to start. My students get to see a wild animal up close, touch their noses, and pet them. They watch a video at the dive shop then they go out and swim with them. If that doesn't make a positive impact on their lives, then I don't know what would."

Dana's idea of a positive impact has grown over the years. Student after student has caught his vision for the environment. Through his newsletter, videos, and classes, he has inspired many dreamers to see the reality of the underwater environment. His trips to Crystal River have opened the eyes of many to the seriousness and awe of endangered species.

One of Dana's watercolors

49 What Are You Waiting For?

In the book, Chicken Soup for the Soul, David B. Campbell has compiled a list. He labels it, "For Me to Be More Creative, I Am Waiting For..." He lists 101 items such as: inspiration, permission, someone to smooth the way, someone to change, the stakes to be lower, a disaster, time to almost run out, an obvious scapegoat, an absence of risk, my ego to improve, next season, my ship to come it, and a less turbulent time.

For Dana the times of turbulence kept him in a whirlpool of confusion for a period in his life. For a period of his life, he only dreamed in frustration of a time when the way would be smoother, or for something in his life to change. Each of these self-imposed excuses held him in the swirling confusion of darkened dreams. Every time one excuse would resolve itself and the storm seemed to subside, another would follow.

Years passed in Dana's life as he waited and watched. Years of wishing and hoping were clouding the clear waters of his vision. Yet, there came a day when he finally said, "Enough". And despite the swirling confusion of his own excuses, he decided to pay the price and move ahead.

Chicken Soup was one of Dana's inspirations to press ahead and pay the price, to ignore the obstacles and press forward into the depths. One of his favorite stories was about a Vietnamese man named Le Van Vu, once one of the wealthiest in North Vietnam. During the Vietnam War the Vus holdings were devastated. He and his wife moved to South Vietnam and actually rebuilt their fortune but lost it all again. On a ship to America Mr. Vu contemplated suicide but through his wife's encouragement he tried one more time. He began again working for two years to buy a cousin's bakery. For two years he and his wife lived in the back room and took sponge baths in the mall restrooms. Today they are millionaires.

The Vus are a prime example of people who could have held on to a list of reasons as to why they were waiting to be more creative.

They could have made their own list: waiting for peace in Vietnam, waiting for another windfall, or wishing circumstances would go their way. They could have stayed in Vietnam, never attaining their dream of moving to America. Instead they chose to "pay the price." They broke out of the whirlpool of confusion and moved into the crystal clear waters of their dream.

Dana, like the Vu's, spent time living in the back room of his store. He was willing to pay the price in order to see his dream become a reality. Night after night he lay alone on his cot surrounded by buoyancy control devices, compressed air tanks, and every piece of his dream. No longer would he sit back and add to a list of what he was waiting for. Now he had taken the steps toward the ultimate adventure.

50 Approval

The rough seas can keep us swirling in confusion. Deep pockets thinking can tell us that we never have enough resources. Dana finally jumped in and decided it was time to at least try to make his dream happen. It wasn't easy. There were times of struggle for survival and even times when the embarrassment of those struggles stung just a bit.

One day in Key Largo Dana remembered that, "We were moving over one of the reefs and I dragged my leg over some coral which I found out later to be Fire Coral and, man did it burn. I tried to tell my buddy what had happened but he did not understand and did not want to turn back. So, I started to the surface and while doing so I almost swam through a school of Barracuda.

Once on the surface I started looking for the boat and finally saw it. I was swimming hard for the boat but didn't seem to be getting anywhere and was tiring myself out. I then realized I was heading for the wrong boat because it looked just like ours. By this time I was tired due to fighting the current and my leg was burning from the coral sting. I was near panic so when I realized I was headed for the wrong boat I started looking for the right one. The waves were about four feet high and I had to wait until I was at the crest before I could see. When I finally spotted it I saw there was someone on the bow waving at me to give the okay sign but I gave the distress signal. They then jumped in the Zodiac and came to get me. I don't have to tell you I was really embarrassed about the whole episode."

He felt like the whole dive was a disaster partly because of what the team would think of him. Approval from others was important to Dana and he eventually realized this was one thing holding him back.

His wife's approval paid a big part in that. Early on Dana discovered a music store that was up for sale. This was back in his airline days when he was more active in his guitar playing. His wife was not excited about the whole idea. It was just too much money, too much time, and too much responsibility. Years later Dana realized that he had developed some stinging resentment toward his wife's disagreement of this issue. Resentments still lurked deep inside of him. If he had it to do again he might have bought the store. But at the time, his wife didn't share his excitement and her approval was very important to Dana. He never bought the music store. It took years before he realized that resentment was a roadblock in opening that business.

Waiting for approval was on his list. Years later he remembered how he and his wife had stood on the beach in the Cayman's talking about his new dream of starting a dive shop. She was 100% behind him and even flew out to California several times to visit him during his eight week PADI training. Her approval helped motivate him to seek his dream. Although she disagreed with the idea of buying a music store she encouraged him in the diving direction. Her disapproval effected Dana's decision to buy the music store, but looking back on it he felt she may have been right about that decision. However, at the time her disapproval was added to his list of roadblocks that hindered his hope.

Sometimes we capture approval and sometimes we run across some fiery coral and get lost in the panic. If we are convinced that our dream is our dream, then we must move on, sometimes without the approval of those around us. History records an endless parade of those who did not instantly win the approval of their peers yet plugged on. The Wright Brothers, Thomas Edison, the Apple Computer boys, and many others were met with those who did not share their vision at first. Yet, they continued on and proved them all wrong.

It's true sometimes we do create an Edsil vehicle which does not win the favor of the crowds. Thousands have forged ahead with their dream only to fall flat in failure. The husband who mortgages his home to invest in a gold fish farm, the woman who earns a Master's Degree in Psychology and ends up as a fast food employee, and young man who invests in an airline which shuts down six months later, are all examples we are too well familiar with.

Dana felt that fear of failure and projected fear of an embarrassing struggle. He never told his wife about that dive at Key

Largo. He said back then, "Hopefully, I will get my confidence back some day and try it all over again." And he did.

51 No Where to Go but Up

On August 19, 1984, Dana's daughter, Angela, had taken up diving and on her first dive to Panama City, Florida, there was a problem. Dana told me about it.

"Visibility can change rather quickly and the current can be strong. On this dive I got turned around and didn't use my compass. When I realized we were turned around I decided we should make an ascent to the surface. Rather than going straight up we ascended in the direction I thought the boat was located, which was correct but with the current running as strong as it was we actually ended up behind the boat. We were swimming against the current, which can be a real problem. Fortunately, our boat had put out a 50' long drift line with a big floatation ball on the end. We surfaced about twenty-five yards behind the float. I felt Angie wasn't a strong swimmer at the time, so I took her hand and started swimming toward the line. Since I was a newer diver, I still wasn't that comfortable in the water, in fact, I was close to panic. Because I knew my daughter was depending on me I kept my composure and we finally made it to the ball. She told me later I squeezed her hand so hard I almost bruised it."

Angela Grubbs Adasme told me her version on the episode. "Yes, it was my first dive and visibility was terrible. We couldn't see anything until we got to the bottom and then the current seemed to get worse. Dad motioned for us to swim back to the boat because it was so bad. I was a strong swimmer but dad held my hand. He always held my hand when I first started diving. The problem was that since we had gone under several other boats had anchored in the area and we finally just guessed which anchor line was ours. We followed it for a ways but then it crossed another anchor line. Dad got real nervous and I remember holding hands as we swam for the boat. We finally made it back okay."

Luckily one of the next dives redeemed this experience. Dana said that, "We were at the next dive site and making our way down the anchor line at a depth of about sixty feet. We were diving on a barge. As we made our way down we could see visibility was better than the first dive and at about the three quarter mark Angie stopped to point out a Manta Ray moving across the bottom. We watched its graceful movements until it was out of site. It was the biggest I had ever seen with about an eight foot span from wing tip to wing tip. And about ten foot from head to tail."

From that trip on, Dana said he started diving more conservatively. He cut down on the distance he covered and stayed closer to the dive area. He told me that, basically he is very cautious of the ocean. It scares him to a certain extent and he has to meet it on his own terms. He says, "If you respect the environment it will make you a better diver. A safer diver"

That same attitude of caution has permeated his plans to pursue his dream of owning and operating his own dive business. There were days when the visibility was terribly turbid. You couldn't see anything higher than your head. His Eastern Airline days were days of poor visibility, days which left him cautious in life's ventures.

Angela remembers those days. "I was seventeen during the Eastern strike. Actually I was on my way to college. When Eastern failed my mother was still working for the Federal government, but because of her auto accident she almost went blind because of detached retina. She was out of work but the government had a program called "leave donations." Mother had used all her leave up, so others would actually donate their leave time to her. That's how we survived for six months until dad finally found odd jobs. I guess I was a little skeptical when dad first decided to go after his dream. After all, we had nothing, and I knew we couldn't even get loans. When I was about nineteen or twenty he got real serious about going after his dream. He had to go for his dream - 'cause there wasn't anything left.

That day in Panama city, Angie and her dad encountered a tough current that stirred up so much silt they could only see the very bottom of the ocean. Diving was worthless that day. There would be no tours of caves or coral reefs. There was even a sense of urgency to get out of there and back to the safety of the boat. The only option left was to go up.

That was the only option left when Dana's life fell apart in the Eastern days. He had sold his houses, lost his career of twenty-one years, and become one of the figures on a fact sheet, the result of America's downsizing. There was nowhere else to go but up. He had hit bottom and he didn't like it.

Sometimes our dreams are all that survive. We can lose our homes, our careers, and even our families in the more tragic situations. But we still have our dreams. Dana's dream never died. He grabbed hold of all that was left and swam for the surface.

Diving in dangerous, life-threatening situations made Dana a more calculating diver. But he had to make a move and do it fast. When Eastern folded he had to make a decision. All around him he saw his buddies from slipping into depression, filing bankruptcies, and even a suicide. Of course there were many who actually made it out of that darkness, and like Dana swam on the best they could. But Dana saw what happened to many others, and he was well aware of what devastation was lurking in murky waters for his own life.

He didn't move quickly. In fact he was very cautious. Already he had experienced the heartbreak of broken dreams and that was the last thing he wanted to happen again. The danger he and his daughter encountered left him a more cautious diver. The Eastern experience created caution as he moved forward. He couldn't just wait on the bottom for help to appear. He grabbed onto the anchor line and began pulling himself toward the light.

Angela told me, "He started out very slow and patient" She also told me how proud of him she was and how he was not only an inspiration to her, but he was an encourager.

"When I was young he always encouraged me to go a little farther. For instance, if I said I wanted to be a nurse he would say, why not a doctor? When he began his dream I was just beginning mine by going to college. Today I am working to become an International Corporate Attorney."

Dana has always been an encourager to his friends. They look at a man who was caught up in the swirl of corporate upheaval and remember a man who had a vision and was willing to go after it.

Tim Durden was one of his buddies from Eastern Airlines. He knew Dana for twenty-seven years. They used to work the ramps together, and Tim said, "Dana is the kinda guy you want in the foxhole with you. We fought the battles and won. I could call him now and tell him I needed something - he'd be there in a minute."

Together they walked the picket lines and watched their careers slip from their grasp. No matter how hard they tried, they could not recapture the twenty-one years of good times and good benefits. "We used to go on trips to Alaska. We'd look for gold and do a little fishing," Tim told me.

Those days were over. The trips to California for a seafood dinner, trips to Alaska, and all the security of a solid career slipped into the whirlpool. Many of his co-workers slipped into that whirlpool of despair, not knowing what their dream was anymore. Most, like Tim and Dana survived, but Dana was one who succeeded in finding his dream. Some, like Tim tried to set up businesses and were met with seasons of distress. Tim got the idea of starting his own landscaping business. He hired his two sons and three or four other young men to work for him. But the dry seasons, slow winter months, and stiff competition stifled his success in that area.

Tim said he had to do something. He couldn't stay on the bottom. "You take your licks and keep on going," he says. He eventually acquired a position with Tamrock and was able to hire Dana in customer service. But, six months after he started, Dana announced to Tim that he was going to start his own dive business. Tim worried about Dana at times. He knows how hard it is to get started in your own business, especially with no money.

"He always wanted to do it, but didn't know he would have to do it without any money," Tim says. But Tim was always there for Dana. He even attained his own Dive Master status and began helping Dana out in the store and on occasional trips. Both Dana and Tim know what it's like to be caught in dark waters. They and many others like them have been on the bottom and discovered that they need to keep on swimming.

52 Survivors

James Robinson was another Eastern Airlines buddy who is still good friends with Dana. For years they worked the ramp together. He, like Tim Durden, had also tried to start his own landscaping business in an effort to help his Eastern co-workers. The problem was they were only making $5-$10 per hour. Today James works as a semi-truck driver carrying produce from California to Miami.

James was one of those guys who used to fly to Fisherman's Wharf with Dana and others. He told me, "The meal was more expensive than the flight itself." He remembers those Eastern Airlines days as good times.

"We worked hard but we had fun doing it," he told me. "Sometimes we really goofed off. A guy would be working and we'd drive past him on one of the tractors dousing him with a bucket of ice water." In the hot humidity of Atlanta's summer heat, ice water was quite a shocker.

He also said, "Over by the freight building there was this little dip that would fill up with water. I would stop my little tractor and make it look like I stalled out. When the guys came to help me I would quick back out and they all got soaked."

James said Dana did his share of fooling around also. One time he came in early with a little black box and taped it up on one of the girders. When the guys were all gathered at the table drinking their coffee Dana nonchalantly pointed up to the box and asked, "What's that?" Then he walked off leaving them in a heated argument about management installing surveillance cameras in their break room.

Those were good times for Dana and his friends. James says, "We spent more time with each other than with our families." They worked together, played together, and eventually survived together. "How did we survive? We had a lot of sharp people there," said James. Dana was one of those people who survived the darkened waters.

James remembers those days well and Dana's dream to press ahead despite the surrounding darkness. "You wouldn't believe how many were divorced, lost their homes, had heart attacks, and ended up in bankruptcies. You wouldn't believe it." But James watched as Dana swam from the turbulent waters into the light of his dream.

There were so many others. Men and women who had invested years of their lives into what they believed was a solid career. This may have been the last residue of a generation that placed their faith in the American dream. They believed that this career would take them into the security of retirement. James Robinson told me they had slipped into complacency. The trips to Fisherman's Wharf, the trips to Alaska and Germany and other parts of the globe seemed to be a permanent part of their future. Little did they know that soon they would become a part of America's downsizing? Many would lose their incomes, their security, and even their health. But for Dana Grubbs and many of his friends, they didn't drown in some silt filled waters of confusion. They had lost almost everything, so there was only one direction they could go. And that was up.

53 A Dream Comes True

The Abyss MR 22 Titanium, the flagship regulator of the Mares line, hangs on the wall along with several buoyancy control devices like the Vector Hl, complete with a 420 Denier nylon bladder. Several pairs of fins like the Plana Avanti Quattros rest snugly against Ergotech and Isotherm wetsuits. The gray booth is no larger than six foot by eight foot. Three of us, Loraine Goard, Dana Grubbs, and me, are sitting across from one of Dana's dealers at the DEMA show. The Mares salesman sports a gray beard and long black hair. He spreads catalogues, manuals, and a current price list in front of us.

Several years before this Dana would not have even been allowed into this booth, let alone full access to the price list. But this time he was a full-fledged Exhibitor/Buyer, fully approved as a member of DEMA.

The first year he attended he traveled to each and every booth and gathered information. He came home with arm loads of information but little stock for his store. He couldn't afford it. The next year he counted his pennies and ordered a few select items for his customers who had placed orders with him. But then business blossomed and the next year Dana excitedly told me he actually attended the show in Orlando, Florida and purchased large orders of stock for his store.

It was in March of 1994 that Dana opened his doors on weekends and evenings. He even came in and opened up during his lunch hours. A bit scared and even a little despondent over his life circumstances, he continued to work full-time, then part-time until January of 1995 when he quit his job and officially opened the doors of "The Ultimate Adventure Dive Center," full time. Money was extremely tight during this time but somehow he survived.

54 Out of the Red

In 1996, his second full year in business, he ended with $147,000, doubling his sales from his first year, and closing in the black. Not bad for someone who started with nothing but a dream? He quickly added that he also had $5,000 in his savings account.

He was also officially certified as a PADI dive shop, which listed him in the International directory and on the PADI home page of the World Wide Web, and he received an extra 5% discount on any supplies he orders from them.

The old 1977 van was still his favorite vehicle. He's was thinking about renovating the inside but he still carried dive equipment around in it for certification classes. The insurance was cheap, it ran great, and it was one of Dana's old friends. Loyalty to his friends and students is one of the qualities that always helped his business to prosper.

The first couple of years were a little scary for a new businessman diving in with nothing. Many businesses were going belly up after just a couple of years. Dana worried about that fact from time to time but continued to follow his dream and listened to the inspiration of those around him.

He told me that, "Before, I wondered if I was going to make it at all.   But, now I know I will. When things get tight I just think of ways to generate more money. I know my business better now. I feel I have more confidence. Back then I knew the dive business to a degree, but I didn't know anything about the retail business. But I learned."

55 Turning Point

His dream was becoming reality.   Income turned from a few pennies to a lucrative vocation that he owned and operated.

"I had to be careful of overconfidence in my spending," Dana said. In the early days every expenditure had to be meticulously accounted for. Spending had to be strategic. Then his income became more abundant and there was the temptation to loosen up, enjoy the things he missed for so long.   There was a temptation to return to the carefree complacency of the Eastern Airlines days. His desire was to continue building his business, so he still held tightly to the cash in his pockets. The trips of Eastern Airlines days had been replaced with diving trips to Florida, the Cayman Islands, and other exotic locations. He enjoyed good restaurants with old friends from Eastern, and his new family of scuba alumni. Dana was even considering buying himself a little house again. Something he hadn't enjoyed since selling his houses during the strike days. Specifically, he was looking for a fixer upper, nothing fancy, just a good deal – or just maybe – he'd buy a small yacht and live on that.

The days of living in the back rooms of his shop were over. With a fond sadness he remembered dreaming on his little cot.   A small television was mounted up in the corner of his classroom for teaching purposes, but he also used it for his evening viewing. He didn't watch much television, but it was there along with a few shelves of books, and his few meager possessions. Only a handful of friends knew the sacrifice Dana was making to bring them into new adventures, and build his dream.   Living among rows of wetsuits, and stacks of air tanks was not really a sacrifice though. It was more of an adventure.

Eventually, he was not only able to move back into a regular house, but also buy himself a nice boat for lazy cruises in the Gulf of Mexico. Now when he slept in small quarters it was on his own boat drifting into the beautiful sunsets of Florida's gulf.

Dana's new boat

56 Vicarious Dreamers

Living in the back room of a dive shop does not fit into the "so-called" normal American social structure. Most of us come home from a nine-to-five routine, slip off the shoes, crash on the couch, and spend the evening with our family. But most of us do not enjoy the benefits of owning and operating our own business. Being devoid of the typical family structure is not a pre-requisite for starting your own business. Not at all. But it may be necessary to make a few changes in the way we live to achieve our dream. Less time with the television and more time working on our dream may be the only way out of the nine-to-five monotonous routine. Monotony seems to breed monotony. We become bored with our life, our career, and our lack of vision, so we tend to lay back and do even less with the little time we have free. Things like television, computer time, social networks, and even reading can joyfully provide an exotic escape to another time and place, but we tend to live vicariously through others experiences. This concept is nothing new. Some people are perfectly content to let others take the Cayman dive trips, to let others begin their own businesses, and even to thrill over the successes of those who finally attained their dreams. Some people will actually sit down and read this book, Dana's experiences, and thrill vicariously over his success, but never get out of their own chair to live it for themselves.

There comes a time when we have to awaken from others dreaming; a time when we comprehend that living it is more fulfilling than watching it. Dana came to that point in his life but he was willing to pay the price. Yet the price was not what he hoped for. It wasn't a deep pocket thing all at once, something he didn't have. And so, he just took it one lap at time. The time he could have spent lounging in his favorite chair, he chose to replace with some positive steps.

57 A Passionate Marriage

Yés, his personal life suffered, but not because of his business. His life slipped into dark waters before he began following his dream, before he opened the doors to his business.   Sometimes, even after he opened his shop he wondered if his social life was out of kilter.

"I had no personal life," he told me. "I worried that I was married to my business at times because everything I did seemed to be wrapped up in it."

When Dana and I talked one day we realized something about his social life. In his younger days he was concerned with raising a daughter, meeting the needs of his family. That's how it is when you are younger. Those things are necessary. But as you get older, the children leave for college and things change. Expenses for kid's glasses, medical check-ups, clothes, and all those other family things begin to level out a bit.   Off course for some, certain health care expenses can increase, and sometimes there is even a drop in income which carries over the strain on the budget. But one thing that seems to become freer is time. Less time is needed for children's school activities, for certain social functions, in other words, our social life moves into a new arena. This is not to say that a young person who has a family cannot start their own business. They are the ones with boundless energy and vision. However, many who are maturing in years are not exempt from new journeys in life. Young or old, it really doesn't matter, if you have vision and step out, it's going to work for you.

Dana, like many Americans was forced into a new direction at a time in life when many want to rest securely on past accomplishments. Dana's daughter was in college. His social life had taken on a whole new direction. Married to his business? In a sense yes. In the sense that he had a passion for what he is doing, and that he loved his work, yes. He enjoyed his work now. No more punching a time clock. No more meeting the expectations of someone else's dream. Now he could spend his time and energy building his own dream.

Dana understood that most of his time was invested in the Scuba business, in trips, and in training. Yet, he also understood that he enjoyed it. It was his passion. Other people sit at home all evening and weekends building relationship with a television. Dana ran a prospering dream, took dive trips, attended plays, movies, and went out to restaurants with his friends. And he had very positive and exciting vision for the future. Many people don't know what tomorrow will bring, have no long term or even short term goals. They are depressed over their future prospects. Dana was far from depressed. He was excited about next week, next month, and ten years from now. He had goals for his future. He knew where he wanted to go with his business.

58 Out of His Comfort Zone

Dana had several major goals for the future. First, he wanted to build a strong enough base in Rockdale County (his dive shop location), so if another dealer moved into the area they would not be able to come in and blow his doors off.

James Robinson told me, "My biggest concern for Dana was that a big competitor would come in and put him out of business. I just hoped he could get secure enough in his footing so that wouldn't happen."

That's exactly what Dana started working on, building that foundation. He did more than just try to set a secure financial base. He didn't just teach students scuba. He built a family. There is a strong sense about Dana that drew you into his store, not just to buy the latest diving equipment, but to see how he was doing. Dana spent time with his family. He loved to talk and was genuinely concerned about the people who walked through his doors. In a world that is customer service care starved, Dana had the right idea This type of business practice was not a simple tactic you learn in a seminar. Dana has always cared about his friends. But when he was on the bottom of a silty sea something enhanced that personality trait. A deep spiritual awakening with his God stirred something deep inside. There was a change in him. Even though he had always had that concern for people, now there was a higher purpose in his life. He attributed his motivation to pursue his dream to his God. Caring about people more than his business was spurred forward and has enhanced his relationships not only with his customers, but even with dealer, and right down to delivery men.

One afternoon I was in the shop and a U.P.S. courier came to the back door with several large boxes. Dana didn't just sign off and dismiss this young man. He addressed him by his name, asked how he was doing, joked about the traffic, and made the young man feel like someone cared about him. That was a refreshing change for me. I had worked in corporate America for years and was callused by the dog-eat-dog attitudes of those around me. Not everyone is out to get on top of the other guys ladder. But there is this subtle polite dismissal of each other's personal life. Who really cares about the co-worker? As long as I do better why should I care about him or her? These attitudes permeate the workplace.

I walk into stores and am met by rude clerks who make me feel like I need to get out of there way as soon as possible. Rudeness and unconcern have bathed the American service centers in a thick coating of "who cares" attitude. That's been one of Dana's secrets of success. People walk in his doors and feel like they are welcome in his home. They walk away with a sense of exhilaration and peace. They want more and are soon enrolled in one of his classes and flying to the Cayman's for a family party.

So, Dana was doing more than focusing on a financial foundation that will not shake in the wind. The cement of his foundation was a genuine concern for those who walk in the doors of his business. People sensed it, felt it, and knew it was true. His friends from Eastern Airlines hung out with Dana like a bunch of old high school buddies. There is a camaraderie there that filters into Dana's business relationships. He was building an army of loyal friends and if another dealer ever tried to blow Dana's doors off, they will have to fight their way through the very people they hoped to win to their side.

However, there was an interesting twist of fate in the year 2000. Another instructor told Dana that he was going to open another store – and put Dana out of business. This shook Dana, a guy who had a deep sense of loyalty to his friends and customers. He had finally found his dream in Old Town Conyers but the waters began darkening.

After thinking about it and searching out options Dana made a change that certainly moved him from his comfort zone, one more time. Out on interstate twenty, a very high trafficked area coming into Conyers from Atlanta, Dana found a new location for his store. It was much bigger and would draw much more attention. It just so happened that the person who built the new store was one of Dana's loyal customers. Dana began renting that new location for his business.

The next hurdle was the fact that Dana did not have enough furnishings for the new store. He was talking to a buddy from

Chattanooga, Tennessee about this and found out that a Sam's Club was remodeling their store.

Dana said, "They gave me all kinds of glass cabinets and slot wall shelving. They were just going to throw it away. That's what they do." The only cost for Dana was a rental truck and his new store was ready to roll.

The plan worked. His business not only survived the other instructor's intent to put him out of business but it grew. He hired three part-time and one full-time employees. "We started expanding our client base, and our trips. Not only were we going to the Cayman Islands, we started trips to Hawaii, Guam, and to the Great Barrier Reef in Australia.

This was a real switch from the 911 days. Dana said that just about sank his business along with so many others in the States. His business was just treading water and he seriously considered closing the doors. "I was just sitting there one day, seriously planning to close the doors in two weeks, and you know how you have one of those moments where you say to God, 'I can't do this anymore it's up to you. And then the next day a customer comes in and buys a full set of dive equipment." That was a turning point for Dana. It is during those dark times, when people lose sight of their dreams, just before break through, that many people turn in their equipment and go home. Dana stuck it out.

Not only did his business set sail and move on the course he hoped for, he actually was able to do more. It was during that period that he was able to take his dive tank to a Wal-Mart parking lot, and with his team, play Monopoly underwater in dive gear for three days. They ended up raising $13,000 - $14,000 several years, for the Miracle League (for sports handicapped participants). This, along with other charity events, like helping with bike races, stirred Dana's passion to not only establish his dream but to help his community.

59 Stronger Sense of Purpose

Dana continued to be very sensitive to environmental issues. His hope was to somehow help educate people to the sensitivity and fragility of our underwater world. The Right Whales and the Manatees were his major focus but he was exploring other avenues also.

He knew a woman biologist who worked in a sanctuary in the Florida Keys. The sanctuary is a protected oceanic location where people dive on a regular basis. It teams with varieties of fish, coral, and numerous ship wrecks. You aren't even allowed to drop anchor in that area for fear of damaging some of the protected wildlife. Dana's idea was to approach a school board, possibly the high achievers program, receive permission to teach a scuba class along with some environmental focus, and then take the students to the sanctuary for their certification. While there the biologist could give them information on the ecological personality of the area.

This would cost Dana nothing. In fact he would make a small profit on the program. But more than that it would help to fulfill his goal of teaching the next generation about our underwater treasures.

"My whole goal," Dana told me, "...is to open eyes to the environmental issues. I mainly want to direct that goal toward the kids, because they are going to be our leaders."

That was one of his goals but he wondered if he wasn't already meeting it to a degree, maybe not with the kids yet, but certainly with the students that passed through his doors. His first several years in business he had already introduced hundreds of students to the Manatees of Crystal River and the cause of the Right Whales. Dana Grubbs first years in his business had been the Ultimate Adventure. Not only had he escaped the nine-to-five rigors of restrained creativity, he had shown countless others the same journey.

60 Crystal Clear Waters

Dana's dream to start his own business was a journey over the years. He came up with creative ideas for beginning his own business and learned through trade and other methods to keep cash in his pockets. He was continually coming up with ideas to build his business. At one point he discovered a simple way to sell more equipment to his students. A hands on approach raised his sales. During the certification classes he and other instructors would simply pull a few choice pieces of equipment off the displays and hand them to the students. If they were discussing ways to clear water from a dive mask, they handed the students a mask and visually explained the process.   If they were discussing the advantages of a certain type of regulator, they passed around that regulator and let the students see it firsthand.

Dana says he avoided a hard sell in these settings. He wanted to avoid pressuring anyone to buy something they didn't want. But he did want to put quality equipment into their hands so they could see the advantages and safety features of such products. And yes, the result was usually another sale. It's just these kinds of creative approaches that made "The Ultimate Adventure Dive Center," become a growing business.

Dana's creativity launched him into a growing market. The dive industry just happened to be an excellent choice for a new business owner. If you were going after a dream, that industry was a great place to dive into. Some reports say it was even surpassing golf in popularity. Dana dreamed, and his dream became a reality. Dana discovered how to achieve the ultimate adventure.

61 His Dream Became His Life

And as three white stretch limousines and a rented van sat waiting outside the Ultimate Adventure Dive Center at 9:00 am on a February morning, Dana's students' milled around excitedly buying up last minute dive items for the trip. Some sat watching a promotional video on Coconut Harbor for one last time before they were to fly off to that Cayman Island destination. Dana had just received a shipment of classy polo shirts with his self-designed logo on the front. Students are trying on and purchasing their own "Ultimate Adventure Dive Shop" shirts.

There was a sense of excitement as all the gear was packed into the van and the divers settled into the limousines. That was Dana's way of capping off a celebration which began with a party at a friend's house the last summer. Jamaican music in the air and shrimp on the barbecue. Over forty people ended up signing up for that trip. By nine forty-five they were on their way.

For one week Dana and his crew dove in the transparent turquoise waters of the Caymans. Visibility could reach up to one hundred feet in those waters. Clarity was a distinction of this diver's paradise. There was something about the Cayman's that cleared a person's thinking and improved their vision. At the beginning of Dana's journey he had come here with his wife and daughter for a weekend of scuba diving. They stayed at a resort called The Spanish Bay Reef. Back then it was called The Spanish Cove.

On the trip with his class, Dana took some time alone and revisited The Spanish Bay Reef. Not much had changed. The breeze was still warm, the waters azure, and the air was still clean and refreshing. He remembered years earlier when he had made his decision. Talking about a dream was one thing, but he finally decided to swim that first lap. It was here, in the Cayman Islands, ten years earlier that he decided to become an instructor and someday have his own dive shop in a place like this. His dream had become crystal clear.   The dive shop was a reality and he was making a living introducing his friends and students to the ultimate adventure.

NEW AGE EXPLORERS
(Music and lyrics by Dana Grubbs)

To dream of adventure and faraway places. To take that first step into
the depths of unknown. To smile at strange creatures as they gaze at
your presence, while you visit the part of our planet unknown.

(Chorus) We're new age explorers starting a journey, a journey to places
unknown and unseen. Your envied by many who can't meet the
challenge, so don't take for granted the wonders you see.

As we visit the floors of our oceans and rivers, to see things that few
ever will see and to smile at the beauty of life as it is given, these are
the things that God gave to me.

(Chorus)
We draw our life's blood from the sea and it's creatures and all we put
back is destruction and death. When the oceans die so goes the planet,
the fate of our future is depending on you.

Dana with one of his many watercolor paintings.

End Note

Dana realized his dream to open and run his own scuba business. He never went into debt and only once took a small short term loan. His business, The Ultimate Adventure Dive Shop, flourished in the Conyers location. Several years ago he sold out, boat his boat, and now lives on the Gulf of Mexico painting, writing, and enjoying life. He also became coast guard certified as a master captain of 100 ton boats and began working some for the owner of Sea School teaching others how to become captains also. At one point he was actually able to take a year off and hike the Appalachian Trail, another dream of his.

When Dana approached me about writing his story I had my own little business for Trade bank International called, The Write Approach. After completing our project a few years passed. It was in that period that I began my own business. "Shepherd's' Purse", is a small non-profit addressing the needs of kids at risk in Ukraine, Russia, and several other country areas. Our main emphasis began with street kids as young as four years old and evolved in to helping orphanages as well.

One day as I was reviewing Dana's project I realized the influence his story had on me starting my own business. So many things he told me actually settled into my journey. At first I thought about birthing this non-profit but wondered where I would get the funds. How would we raise supporters? What about office expenditures? A thousand questions kicked in that deep pocket thinking. Before I even opened one door I followed in Dana's steps when he looked into beginning his dream and realized he had no resources for such a lofty goal. But then – Dana's voice kicked in and I thought, "What is one thing I could do today?" It was at that point I decided to make space on my home desk and start a small newsletter. Every step of the way was a challenge for me but over a period of time it all became crystal clear. I made sacrifices such as a home office, figured a way to finance my trips by taking teams over with me, and numerous other ideas.

Dana's ideas aren't necessarily mind blowing new concepts. Yet, they are simple reminders and encouragements to just get up off the couch and see what we can do with what we have – today.

Author – Michael Wetzel

ABOUT THE AUTHOR

Michael Wetzel began his writing journey in 1985 after taking a class called "Writing for Publication" at the Milwaukee Area Technical College. During that class he sold his first article to "Fur-Fish-Game" magazine on bear hunting. This began publication of over eighty articles and various news pieces.

He has written articles in the Sunday supplement for "The Lansing State Journal", and had a column in "The Edgerton Earth, a regional newspaper in Ohio.

Most recently his book, "Shepherd's Purse – For the Forgotten Ones", was published by New Creation Press. This is the story of children-at-risk in Russia and Ukraine. After the break-up of the former Soviet Union literally millions of children escaped abuse due to the rise in alcoholism or were just abandoned to the streets or orphanages. This is the story of how God led Michael to begin a small ministry to help. Order at: www.shepherdspurse.org

Over four-hundred poems have been written and published in several booklets. "The Prodigal's Journey" is based on the Biblical prodigal son and Michael's own journeys. He also has a collection of poems coming soon.

"The Prodigal's Journey ", is based on Michael's own journey through a dark period in his life, and the street kids of Ukraine and Russia.

"The Ultimate Adventure" is the story of one man's dream, Dana Grubbs, to begin his own scuba diving business and the lessons he learned along the way in starting up a small business with no money or resources.

All books are available on Amazon.com

www.ingramcontent.com/pod-product-compliance
Lightning Source LLC
Chambersburg PA
CBHW051507170526
45166CB00001B/428